THE THREAD

BY STEPHEN SANDY

POETRY

The Thread: New and Selected Poems
Thanksgiving Over the Water
Man in the Open Air
Riding to Greylock
Roofs
Stresses in the Peaceable Kingdom

LIMITED EDITIONS

Vale of Academe
The Epoch
The Hawthorne Effect
End of the Picaro
The Difficulty
Japanese Room

PROSE

The Raveling of the Novel

TRANSLATION

Seneca's *Hercules Oetaeus* (as *A Cloak for Hercules*)

THE THREAD

New and Selected Poems Stephen Sandy

LOUISIANA STATE UNIVERSITY PRESS   BATON ROUGE   1998

Copyright © 1971, 1982, 1989, 1990, 1993, 1994, 1995, 1996, 1997, 1998
    by Stephen Sandy
All rights reserved
Manufactured in the United States of America
First printing
07 06 05 04 03 02 01 00 99 98   5 4 3 2 1

Designer: Laura Roubique Gleason
Typeface: Janson Text
Typesetter: G & S Typesetters, Inc.
Printer and binder: Thomson-Shore, Inc.

Library of Congress Cataloging-in-Publication Data

Sandy, Stephen.
    The thread : new and selected poems / Stephen Sandy.
        p.   cm.
    ISBN 0-8071-2257-2 (alk. paper). — ISBN 0-8071-2258-0 (pbk. :
alk. paper)
    I. Title.
    PS3569.A52T48   1998
    811'.54—dc21   97-47291
                                                          CIP

Most of the poems herein have been selected from: *Stresses in the Peaceable Kingdom*
(Houghton Mifflin, 1967), copyright © 1960, 1961, 1962, 1963, 1964, 1965, 1966, 1967 by
Stephen Sandy; *Roofs* (Houghton Mifflin, 1971), copyright © 1971 by Stephen Sandy;
Riding to Greylock (Alfred A. Knopf, 1983), copyright © 1966, 1971, 1972, 1973, 1974, 1976,
1977, 1978, 1979, 1981, 1982, 1983 by Stephen Sandy; *Man in the Open Air* (Alfred A.
Knopf, 1988), copyright © 1973, 1974, 1982, 1983, 1984, 1985, 1986, 1987 by Stephen
Sandy; and *Thanksgiving Over the Water* (Alfred A. Knopf, 1992), copyright © 1992 by
Stephen Sandy. Some of the poems first appeared in the following limited editions: *Caroms*
(Groton Press, 1960); *Mary Baldwin* (Dolmen Press, Republic of Ireland, 1962); *Destruction
of Bulfinch's House* (Identity Press, 1963); *Japanese Room* (Hellcoal Press, Brown University,
1969); *End of the Picaro* (1977); *After the Hunt* (Moonsquilt Press, 1982); *To a Mantis* (Plinth
Press, 1987); *The Epoch* (Plinth Press, 1990).
    The author also makes grateful acknowledgment to the editors of the following periodi-
cals, in which some of the poems, or versions of them, first appeared: *American Poetry Re-
view*, *Antioch Review*, *Atlantic*, *Bennington Review*, *Boulevard*, *Carleton Miscellany*, *Chelsea*,
Grand Street, *Green Mountains Review*, *Harpers*, *Harvard Magazine*, *Horns of Plenty*, *Hudson
Review*, *Identity*, *Iowa Review*, *Michigan Quarterly Review*, *Minnesota Review*, *Nation*, *New
England Review*, *NER/BLQ*, *New Republic*, *New Yorker*, *Paris Review*, *Partisan Review*, *Poetry*,
Rising Generation, *Salmagundi*, *Silo*, *Southern Review*, *Southwest Review*, *Truck*, *Visionary
Company*, and *Yale Review*.

The paper in this book meets the guidelines for permanence and durability of the Commit-
tee on Production Guidelines for Book Longevity of the Council on Library Resources. ∞

Contents

from *Thanksgiving Over the Water*

American Days: New Poems

FROM
Stresses in the Peaceable Kingdom (1967)

Wild Ducks

Nine mallards amiably swim
the stream's treadmill. Sedate,
intent; bills front, they form
a V unmoving as kites

swimming the unseen wind.
Upstream they go together;
they glide as if upstream
some hand guides them there.

With button eyes not looking
they move, unmoved, in the pull
of taut, positioning strings,
the hand's extended will.

The Woolworth Philodendron

Among the plastic flowers one honest one
graced Woolworth's floor: a real dodo in a green-
house of smilax and excelsior, a sort of proto-
gewgaw, if you please, it was so dada
in that museum of small cheers,
leaves snapped and torn by the sheer
relentless legs of ladies foraging
for comfort; in a plastic pot, the real thing.

Suspecting it alive, I brought it home.
Five months it sulked in a leafless dream;
through grillings by the daily sun it never broke
its dimestore trance, tight-lipped as rock.
And now it is April in the pliant bones and strange
to note the beaten juices fuse and plunge:
a green prong spirals up to the blaze, unplugs
revenge for ladies' grazing and ungrateful legs.

The shoppers' world is washed away—how fine
to see my green tooth cut the sunshine
and make a brittle pact with the sun's plan!
But it's more than the tender gesture of a jungle vine.
I watch it coil to careful multiplicity
through my weeks of boring work; I have begun to see
a careless wildness, long-leaved and green,
mesh with dark plots implicit in the sun.

Hunter's Moon

An airborne dragon-
fly brash with first frost
buzzed me where I lay
in the open, still,
considering a
juniper lap and
vein the clouds;
                    floating
like seaweed or a
mote down the eye's film,
he stained the sky with
four mica-seamed wings,
just able to hold
on to his outrigged
eyes, spying—a head?
—a stone?
                    Circling or
in the sunless air
coasting he hovered
the wing whirr missing
flaking, taking me
again—his insect
candor!—and again
for a window, a
door, a sun-banked stone,
any warm thing.

Hiawatha

1

False dawns
defunct as Jefferson and Monticello.
Skins of falcon wrapped in bladder, stiff
(brown paper, twisted), tied with sinew. A mauve
snuff box: "European manufacture."

They lie
locked in a case misty with handprints. Pale
lares and *penates* of tribes gone
to our reward. The painted bits call up
my bringing up in Minneapolis
(*city of water*, Ojibway & Greek),

haunt of Hiawatha
and his Minnehaha, whose stream once fell
dark past our home to its thundering fall.

There were no words between us then
when I followed my brother. Behind our fall
in the hollow we hid laughing,
quaffing the yellow mist; once,
dizzily bracing, gave streams of urine to the torrent.
Our selves. In that shade, shreds of sunlight and water
spattered us, held us. In that place we
were of it: outside was make-believe. Then

sun alone webbed our eyes; the misty
light walked on our legs.
We passed that sun-fired wall, boulder-
heavy, heavy enough to drag a boy down

in its scathing heave. Yet the sinewy whirl
skirling headlong from ledge lip high
up there fell inside to a soft
mist of embrace. Thought drowned in that grasp; we
                                        were
there, was all, contained by that cave, laid out
on the tawny stone. The white mane spumed light
into our stringy bodies: we shivered
sharing light's movement in our flesh.

And the Indian.
The Indian gave in
gave up his most secret possessions.
Successful men, their hands in the till of the land,
gave up that fall. They
raised a dam's apron nine miles upstream:
a lake for a land development. Real
estate came first:
                        water grew less.
                                        Finally
only a stream, like bathwater from a tap,
roped down from the fall's brink.
                                Then nothing.
Moss fumbled
over the rocks by the pool below; fish
rummaged in algae; the hollow
behind the fall, a dent bashed in the cliff
whose sandstone, worn by the force of waters,
sagged in creased swags like the belly
of a woman of many children.
The glen that had pooled fallen waters
was a rose of dust.
                        Then
an icicle.
            We woke
cold to a perilous morning, one

beginning of us gone, a dream
which we'd been wakened from.

Upstream, two-by-four
wickerworks stapled the meadows;
barrows of formstone under the drifts
waited building weather. Blades
scored the tranced waters.

2

Under the silver maples the young leaves
have strewn grapes of sunlight. Ten yards
upstream from the brink, leached gray and smooth now,
the Indian's monument stands. I see him,
proud prince of the Onondaga
(Hiawatha, *maker of rivers*)
toting his princess forever; still he goes
over the dead creek bed: crisp leaves, pale stones.
His bronze arms hold her high so her toes
won't dip in the stream he fords alone
in the stream which is no longer there:
he walks where a mayor decreed he should,
a debris of benches, a brawl of picnics now.

Where the wind works patchwork napkins, and Saran
wraps wad at roots of elm trees, this Indian

commends to our Polaroid snaps, our immortal poses,
what was of what never was; himself.

Somehow: these relics got arranged here
—the sacred shell, worn by long use
in sacred ceremony; diminished skins
of martins, the meaningless holy pebbles,

the whole bag of pitiable tricks,
lean fetishes, these tinder bits, these
are some inheritance—not less
for lack of guarantees. We held

we held
that Hiawatha retained a nobility
which our minds had fashioned for our lives.
He was the instance on earth of essences
we held to have been the possible

condition of our lives.

    Hiawatha, tubercular, alcoholic,

    knew every lake and lair of game,
    guided my father on fishing trips,
    drank whiskey round the fire with the men,
    who chipped in twenty for the tip.

    One night, the winter of '56, he set
    home from the tavern, home from the hill.
    One last pull in the snow: then sleep.
    They found him brittle, immobile

    as bronze Hiawatha bearing his Penelope
    over the leaves in the park where children
    peer in casual disbelief at the god
    we made of what

    we most deeply believed, the sign of a profitable
    treaty with wildness; of something
    within, beyond us, too essential
    ever to be entertained in life.
                          The man

and his woman still cross the essential
stream of our youth, the stream which is
not there: for us, for him.
                              A death,
a truth, a childhood of us gone.

Teacher has told them another tale
the eyes of the children say:
they came for the fall, and it's not there.
But the boys accept, demand response; two
let stones fly, aimed at goldfish. Far-off
the plash is scarred by the suburb bus horn's squall.

And schoolchildren ramp each spring now
at the lip of the glen by that fall,
holding breath as their glances flow
over the rock ledge like dazzled water.
Here for the fall, they bridle, daunted, as gazes
slow into nothing, nothing but air.

The Circular in the Post Office

1

In a field in Maryland
in a vacuum cleaner box taped shut
        this boy was found.

The authorities not sure
of even his age—no trace of who
        his parents were,

no clothes, no name—just marks
of strangulation. They found his stare,
        his teeth, his sex

and now in post offices
on bulletin boards and city desks,
        all public places,

his naked faces stare
above the weight, the exact time
        when found, and where.

2

I turn away, but turn
again to watch this boy among
        the "Wanted" men.

I try to imagine the life
that ended up by hanging here.
        His photograph

has caught him once for all
on the wall crowded with crooks seen
             "Front" and "Profile."

Like a brown bag you pop
his paper skin is flattened there
             and shrivels up.

The black around his eyes
seems char, as if his life flared out
             in two quick cries

exhaling like a balloon
its substance, like a member spent
             and wilted down.

             3

He had no father, mother
to call to in that night, and now
             there is no answer

to the authorities' demand
for parents. He sleeps among dark trees
             in unploughed land

and finds no father, mother.
The clue is a blanket round his knees;
             there is no other

in a field in Maryland
in the vacuum cleaner box taped shut
             where he was found.

The state's police declare
his height, his weight, the color of
          blue eyes, blond hair.

But all the authorities
who can't detect his killer, or what
          his name might be,

admit they cannot say
who thrust him into the world, or who
          forced him away.

The Destruction of Bulfinch's House

8 Bulfinch Place, designed and lived in by Charles
Bulfinch, architect of the National Capitol; for years a
tenement, it is razed to make way for government
buildings.

His graceful swag blocks catch the eye,
but senses stall at whiffs of death . . .
antique cosmetics . . . urine . . . sweat
ooze from ruined windows and try
to grasp some walker through this breath
of air they won't give in to yet.

Outside, next door where Bulfinch built,
a silver nameplate on the door
I find caked black with sooty scum.
I pry at it. I rattle the bolt . . .
A woman calls from an upper floor
at her dog to stop. She strikes me dumb.

Inside Bulfinch's hollowed home
the nose goes gaga at more smells . . .
damp char and rust . . . here, haggard sheets
still on the beds—just risen from.
These personal effects excel
the remains outside in mangled streets:

mauled rooms bleed trash, not yet resigned
to emptiness. As if for a bomb
they fled—too rushed to pack—yet more
than glad to leave their lives behind,
as if not miffed to head for some
final occasion in the shirts they wore.

Nothing's removed but every sink!
A dumbbell rests by uncanned food;
and paper breasts, akimbo, boss
the room, beaming with lipsticked pink.
Only those scrawls of solitude
survive this small, survivable loss:

and yet I poke this man-made mess.
I guess what souls this mess has made
—and grub for a Bulfinch souvenir.
Here's one!
                    Here's worth beneath the dross!
A handworked ceiling—plaster frayed
and cracked—but a lace of wreaths still clear.

Watch it! My grime goes white as the sieve
of a ceiling rains. Some witch up there
swears out. A hoarse bass spurts, *you go
to hell.*
          I see it's time I leave,
copping a doorknob and wondering where
in hell you tell people to go.

Can

I found a sharp and jobless can,
now only fit to cut and scold.
It rang its tongueless gong of tin:
    rattling, rattled, cold.

Each time I kicked the thing its shout
echoed a bright, unopened youth.
Looking for work, it tossed about,
    one spiteful, jagged mouth.

Only a bent tin soldier, lame,
it went off crying to hold new food
(louder but lighter than it came),

    no heft, no shine, no good.

Her River

It took all week, I don't know what it means.
Sun red and sexual and gone and I'm alone.
They will not tell me and their words are wrong.
Their helps are evening journals on the stream;
The branches broken like leaves along the storm.
This fish is tied in the bottom of the river.
And people are so careless with each other.
The rope in my throat, I don't know what it means.

It flowed all month, I don't know where it goes.
I broke my glasses, my feet go under snow.
The shell of that nut is horny but it's warm inside.
The lily pads bred corn-smut when they died.
O the moon weeps because it is white and gentle
And the wet cat claws me in the cradle of my arms.
The things they do, so careless with each other.
It takes so long I don't know what it means.

I let it ring and ring and do not answer, let
it ring and slice my ear drums, patiently.
The earth winces when they pull the cut elm down.
I burned my clothes. Grass grows in the sawdust place.
And up the pine the crane clings in the rain,
Huddled against the trunk; sap clings to feathers.
Somewhere is no crowding; and there were children.
Things careless with each other take so long.

Celtic Law

The Lady's dispensation:
      to give the gold ring
      and a good harp
      to the lesser singer.

And his allegiance to her:
      to sing
      .with meet quiet
      up to three songs:

Not disturbing his Lord's company,
      the Lord,
      or the Lord's
      Singer while he sang.

Watersheds

The upper lake, by its
    convulsing trickle
fell, the packing culvert's torsions heaved white
water crumbling, and hourly became
the lower lake: the upper unaware
of its depleting of itself or what
deep transmigration inadvertently
    was making there,
    under the road between,
as a slow seeping;—to what succeeding
body of water it would give itself.
    That afternoon
    in the late year's sleek light
both lakes looked gravid, blank with a sluggish
dignity; neither by the least ripple
acknowledging it was becoming more
or less than itself. The upper might have
been a father, tightlipped, grim to see his
    son change body,
    his kindred wax and wear
his old sinews in the sun, as a young
spore flies the flag of its diminished seed.
    Spray lathered and leapt up
    atilt and strewed itself
down gullies of light; coiled to gloss the air.
The grave bodies, the tumble vying with
sunlight between, made a fit relation
in that serious process: no party
acting agent, each into predicate
    of its nature
    as the seasons followed.
But perhaps that upper lake (as father)
had no sense, had no need to acknowledge:
    for it, from deep
    springs or distant hills, was
being refreshed with a clearer liquid.
And the lake below, the darker waters

screened by the hills from the declining light,
were fulfilling themselves, already were
spilling themselves below the surface
      at some mouth not
      recognized, not charted,
to the valleys below, all the valleys
and plains beyond, and to a distant sea.

New England Graveyard

Back of the church the busy forsythias bow
and scrape to May and all these blessed stones
stiff in their careful finery of words;
the mess of markers makes me go and browse.

Somehow the blocks of slate and marble hate
to be cut and carved to the dimensions
of Mary Monday's age and her virtues.
At heart they hurt to be made literate
and they are rebelling, fast as they can,
shedding an edge, a letter, as they go
—a year, a part of a skull, a bone—
it hurts them to stand so long for this
kind of death not theirs. Fast as they can
they are leaning away from their duty
and look down longing for the warm sod.
The prides and fears they stand witness to,
the ladies and gents, are only whimsy now.
They cease to reflect that wary pride
the flesh beneath them took in lying down.
To the last date line and death's-head stare,
the legend reads, "There! I've done it!"
But these are only beginning,
the blocks of shale forget their lines
letting the sunlight and rain divide
and subdivide their veins and bone.
They do not care, they only feel
an unnatural heaviness, tottering so
in the hot light. They long to be off and away,
they toss and jibe in the sun;
a whole regatta of black sails, they are sailing away
over the lumpy green yard of time, and never

coming about for home until they capsize
turned turtle by boys from Central Square.

Tired of holding—they are tired of holding up;
their always-leaning makes me hold my tongue
and sit with them awhile. We heave
our shoulders, or our shadows, on the mounds,
while under the hills, memorials more fine
lie lip to paper lip
                    and keep their impossible word.

A Dissolve

The dream is tamed.
Fabulous bison of hunters'
memory, pumiced bone.

The idea
takes shape, virgin white pine logged, stripped
clear to Minnesota.

It all dissolves,
the dying straggle in green fjords
of tall grass. They veer off,

the horses dying.

Light in Spring Poplars

A populace—but
of one blood. Contagious,
one, the sun
in the white poplars flared, radial, foamed

infecting through, when
up cold marches of the
slow season
buds caught; waxed in the pealed light, as the sun

on far flaked waters
was one husked candle
furled to light
others;—the gold buds many, but one flame.

Stresses in the Peaceable Kingdom

1

Dahlia's gold explosion,
Queen Anne's lace in seed: wide

lattice, brittle grid: where
sleep divides, divides
                    ripe
melon ripening still, a
fullness splitting
                    elders
dancing, "remembering
but not affecting youth"

vegetables smiled, and
Adam saw fervor, saw

his age a smoulder wrought
and rallied by the sun.

2

The Garden of Eden,
remember, was only

a garden to Adam
as he trod long shores
                    the
fallen breaker, the white
sand, the green wall of trees:

then Adam wandering
toward his evening, released

upon the host his earth,
and time: first companion

limits! For Adam, for
atom, bursting forth, an

energy unleashed upon,
informing the waste world.

Et Quid Amabo
Nisi Quod Aenigma Est

Then watching the unposed beggars pose
I saw the subjects that occasion offered him
doubtless never intrigued the master
as they intrigue us:
Harvest, the Kermesse, Justitia, Skating.
He took down suffering—and those insanely
rush-hour comments on where some action was—
first as a means to chaffer his betters, those
lumpish onlooker burghers, too often viewed
at a distance.
        Obviously, though, he was
moved by dolts; the highly sketchable maimed;
the cloaks in which you feel fleas mincing
and see where rats, by night, nibble. Just what
inner occasion let him see things—
        things as they were—
is not clear; only that he needed them.

Take "Blind Peasant, Begging"—the dazzled eye,
wild stare of a winter deer begging food or
safe passage from where he's been cornered. But
smiling, incongruously—a wily smile,
up-to-no-good, you think. Yet the whole body
in rapt and freehold peace. Not ignorance, this
indifference to the pains which make him up.

        Or take all these little fellows
clumping about with hats over their eyes
all looking squashed, like dwarfs, chin flush with chest
and neck sinking its root in shoulder thew:
this swirl of dying dancers might have been called
"Ataraxy Among the Accident-Prone"
or "Survival Through Indifference, as seen
in the Peasants of Breughel."
        After so many
scrapes as patently planed their knotty faces
the living showed through; lives, like their profiles,

gathered a certain definition from
cold fires and dry trenchers. Chill days grew light
and marvelous when each got circumscribed,
like three-time losers the second time around.

I thought of others: people I knew, whose smiles
stolidly flickered like home movies; some who
displayed lapsed attitudes, say, toward going out
in the rain (without coat or rubbers) all day;
the crowded minds, decreeing against the crowd,
or sailing alone at night in rising weather.

                  Madness may well
be a crowded mind. But fury comes to the
stripped life. The soul that would survive its strife
grows
       accident-prone, carefully careless
with its flesh.—Not the stink, taste,
the sore of having been so wanting long,
the dizzy or the colic of haste

                 it is the *against*,
the gainsaying of the hap bidding
hapless to death's gain: deathward, weighted,
wearied sunless, the cringing, the hulk strange
of a presence, a space change, a win time dons
when you gag in the gorge of the timing,
the falling, the false surrender:
sleeping in doorways, sailing alone at night,
who wryly bear their limps, their abdominal
pains, all mornings after, hanging and hanging,
lousy shirts, the pocked forearm, and scarred wrist.

Home from the Range

I can hear the dour howl of far
breakers from sea shells held to my ear

and deep from my skull I hear the
same small, inveterate tolling
—I've come of age!
                    America,
a screened knowledge;
                    the bad duty
serving one's country.
                    My head is,
the waste is, not clear; is a sound
rings like the sea in my ear,
                    rings:

        "Minuscule nerve ends of the inner ear
        abraded by a rough sound," the doctor said,
        "you will be deaf in the highest ranges;
        no matter, you won't miss everyday sounds;
        hear talk, the usual noises, music . . ."

"Flag is up—Flag is waving—Flag

is down."
            The bolt slides home in my
head a slender explosion—

but a fist's distance from the ear.

                    *

Waters rolling, the sound of war,
heavy traffic on wet pavements
the far-off highways
                    the plains, the
straddled sanctuaries
                    the fast

wildnesses hooped, roped like
                              horses
being broken, the lasso of
highway, concrete belt, the sing of
vans
        cars escaping into space

such as Merton and his brothers
hear from their dark dormitories
Kentucky nights . . .

                              *

                      The sound, the guns
(said the Fort Knox private who knew)
was the sound of the sea
                      heard inland—
heard as immortal agony
as galactic matter earthbound . . .
of God
        in his generations
wild. Crashing against the shore of

our flesh, womb-wrought curl of ear,
natal memorial, chalice
of delicate lobes:
                      "Ready on
                      the Right
                              Ready on the Left
                      Ready on the
                              FI—RING LINE . . ."

                              *

Nothing
        nothing will clear this waste;
guns of unlearned knowledge toll.
                              Arms
hold me with a light GI ring;

a slight ear-plug, always in place.

At Gethsemane
                Merton hears
the guns of Fort Knox. The ring of
sea
          the sound of the traffic down
the inmost canals of our life.

*

Srrrrriiiinng—
          "Always
be deaf in the highest ranges."

Wintering in a Building
Once an Ice-House

Neatly reprieved from ice, this
    house part ice-house still:
sawdust-packed studs keep snug the
    space they once had held cold.
Outside, sparrow and junco
    worked a crude feed stand
convinced that I, inside, would
    not preach to them. They
lacked time.
                Still, they took their time!

    Junco and sparrow
of black, boreal forests
    peered equatorward,
possessionless, in at my
    unseasonably
temperate zone of comfort.
    They did not mind me
staring back, marveling at
    their quick regardless
isolation from their deaths,
their timeless song,
timeless hunger of their cries!

    I am rooted, I
perish in their eyes like summer
    under my warm clothes!
—hang on, hang like a spider
    guarding the space he's
wired off to supper from
    —or like the winch nailed
to this ice-house gable, which
    (strutted to swing-lift
clean-sawn blocks from the cleared lake
    inside)
                hangs there still.

FROM
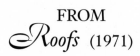 (1971)

Roofs

Sewn straw, exact pattern. Fields of rice-sprigs
evenly set, a mile of herringbone tweed.
The town, a sea of gunmetal, fish-scale tiles.

By morning each floor a casserole of pillows,
coverlets, comforters, towels: flown nests. Imprint
of bodies, fading. They fold the beds away,
the room waits empty all day.
                         All day the bodies
circle, leaving no impression on each
other. Tooled in the foundry of the streets.
School-caps, factory-packed subway, miracle train:
one territorial imperative,
an emperor's.
                    On his platform one yard square
perched on a roof that slopes in waves of tiles
up toward other tiled cascades, the karate student
for hours does running in place, deep knee bends
on his surfboard perch. All his free time to make
his body efficient, tight, exact, rising
and falling, mint piston pumping in its shaft.

November Larches

Maple and elm have done
   with their gold and their
      mulberry, yet

still this gleam comes, back, fur
   in the fogged windshield;
      passive;   passing.

This one wet golden gray
   they come up: a slow
      burn, nightlights low

in the dimmed house of frost.
   There is reason in
      remembering these

larches yellow, young, come spring:
   seeing how low they are
      turned for winter.

A Short Account of the Japanese

Still in step, arm in arm, the Japanese
   do nothing, not even
      skiing, alone.

Sailing them up like swallows the ski lift
   locked to one pace
      controls the spaces

between the bodies floating. Such a gift
   must have been invented
      by the Japanese!

Boys and girls wrapped carefully in sportive
   uniforms, like gifts strewn
      in the tinsel snow,

they plummet and traverse and do snowplow
   turns together, never
      falling and never

stepping from line: until at last they go—
   whoosh!   cartwheels—losing their
      balance together.

Prince Genji's Dance and Triumph

1

Could Genji, if he lived,
tell us what
Heian gentlemen did, beyond their doing it?
That Genji danced before the emperor
who wept to see such grace
while the sun set
beyond those pillared wavering sleeves,
such grace
as might remind the cloistered king
of sadness
deep as any bumpkin's
plodding His Grace's fields
slowly toward animal death. What man
might breathe so, so
thoughtlessly,
but to begin
again, as Genji, the different tempo?

What is your maple leaf that streams,
red tag of passing, ours,
that bolts toward seed, wind, the dead
harvest on bone-white stone,
this court?

2

Would they speak of such
wary abundance and stark
gentleness, surfeit
of self? And the familiar
stroke of sword? Can I know
in my own flagging
my own? The art to keep:
and what strange art is that

which only dallies and does not give,
a dust which grows on life?

How shall he kill
the part of him that kills?
Someone must make the gesture granting freedom.
May he come
raising his hand
sowing like sunlight after storm
freedom from fear
in the ruler's heart!

The sun falls in long shadows of the acacia saplings
across the field that fresh wind wimples.
Beyond the speed of light
warm across my hand
lies the void. We may not
kill what kills us. And such
knowledge is just bearable
to an emperor bearing all his pride,

man squeezing the planet from his life
as if to purify his chalky bones
of the rich waters of his soul.

Work

Kneeling here, writing:
"rainy season" at a low
table. Legs tucked,
tingling;   fresh lilacs stuck down
a tub of soda water.

I came to hate my
books. But that was not needed
either. Hydrangeas
let their blue sky-patches out
easily, by any wall.

Intersections

To begin with he loved this
jammed intersection of the present
this neon scrawl against cloud gleaming

as that concourse, distant and
unending, stars;   this laden crossing
of present and present, apartment

with deepest perspective, the
distance between mountain and mountain
flame and flame, soon slowly furnishing

one point, one hallowing space
of arms outreaching: and he embraced.
Whose bodies gathered light by touching.

                    *

Streaming below, away, back
the townsfolk and cornsilk countryside.
The sun dead ahead, not rising yet,
red coal in coral cloudbank . . .
Alaska. Then the mad hazard of
sparkles, Japan at random on black
air below.
                    A shy girl
her white American wedding gown
folded under the seat worried and
crammed, as for an exam,
thousands of miles for her groom's language—
and life—who met her down there;   drove her
to Hitachi City and
closed her with her oboe (she showed it
to me) and an in-law to teach her
proper tying of sashes.

I see you zoned on his matted floors
abandoned to a strict loving;   tied

to the pruned countryside and
factory siren. You practice your
oboe: the company symphony.

*

The caged squirrel spins his wheel.
The plumed rooster, stepping on his cage
as if plucking the metal threads, stands
where kamikaze taxis
scream cage-left;   cage-right, preoccupied
and uniformed, students press ahead.

And whatever the café
a tank glooms there, glass cell for fish, gold
carp and black;   sleek ghosts, diminished, of
forgotten geisha hovering
in the soft light of their floating world.
A film of fins, erotic silks, wafts

still water: bred thoroughly
in fantasy;   able to move, but
where, in such rooms? Their ancient nature
canceled slowly, need spun out
with care. The harmony that nature
so long attended, no longer here.

*

He slaps her freely—in dreams
—and probably she exercises
the same right when he has not behaved.

Mostly they love to discourse
with friends of their own sex. Silence may
be the deep conversation. Sometimes.

But if this so pure, wordless
exchange fails, then small talk (the smaller
the better) is pure delight for a

whole night. The sense of play, of
the whole trivia all stream upon;
that the spontaneous, *ludens*, keeps

always! Thus the sumptuous
useless strife with style, one lasting game
that all, engulfed by fashion, play.

For one night to be decked out
almost a Heian lady—almost—
is one thesis, one antithesis,

if mind is body, body
mind. So they play cards each night till two.
Ancient children, permission granted.

*

In Chiba-ken the eldest
son, at high school, made this of himself.
First among his fellows he excelled
as his father before him
in martial art;   the judo black belt.
Enticed to the temple precincts then

classmates in a band beat him.
The front teeth gold now, the father warned
do not resist. Elsewhere the winner
in running and in throwing
lies dead at the clenched hands of teammates;
chorus singing comment, holding hands.

*

No flies even in August
and at curbs now the frilled magenta
cabbage replaces summer flowers.

It is winter. As ever
Japanese flowers hustle the eye
but have no smell. On the packed corner

the vendor offers maroon
apples cantaloupe-size, and price;   what
a fine shoulder, that! At last I see

how this diminutive strives,
may be strong;   grown strong, capable of
heaviest burdens. We say "*History*

of Space Travel is well worth
reading."—1776,
I think, and all that "strategy for

peace." Each semantic circus!
Each winner must turn in his trophy
on leaving the auditorium.

What use is it? Now even
apples are pollinated by hand
in the great orchards of Himeiji.

*

Or Mishima: "should these things
pertaining to spirituality
submit to the temporal? Once done

this can be an example
for others," wrote holy Becket. This
technology, the doom of Nippon.

Experts in adversity
you have looked hard, exacting too much
of nature. For example the branch

of a normal, blooming plum
you see not bunched, sun-reaching, aligned
with others, as in plums photographed

ever so artistically
in Trieste or California,
but as pruned, by hand in life, by mind

in eye, to zigzag so and
so: as if a painter or the pained
gullets undernourished for ages

by a short food supply and
a strict Bosatsu, decreed that this
world should not go scot-free;   and to keep

nature from making the mind
a monkey with the jitters, bind this
green world (of petals holding home wide,

straining to call bees through days),
feed it on discipline, and water.
So they teach, a cold dream is this world;

so this teaching would enjoin
man to mind Southern Paradise, a
jade mountain;   and saplings to favor

elegant disillusion.

*

Here, lying awake in this
fireless house I hear Ann now;   I
don't know where she lives, how far she comes.
She comes with winter sunrise,
the rumble of first commuter trains;
in the white smock and socks and slippers
forlorn she thrashes with our
mess, the dirty dishes and dirty
clothing. The household sleeps;   her noises
rouse me;   but they hold me, still.
We do not belong to ourselves;   even
the night soon belongs to a morning.

Mr. Reed of Martha's Vineyard

They found his kayak but they never found him
I thought for no reason sitting in Tokyo
                     eating my shrimp rice and bean sprouts
watching the bulge of a five-months-pregnant woman
standing, waiting to get my seat.

Why do people I find myself asking
forget this needed thing—to be
generous to themselves?
                        You, Alex,
the carefully gardened, wind-combed hill,
I remember the ample light-swept spaces
of the clean house he built for himself up there,
who tossed for a week or so while he became
debris, strewing some floor of the Atlantic.
                     It was winter, I think,
and he was a good swimmer.

The woman has found a seat. These Japanese
are so patient
                    and expect so little, except good manners,
not comfort even.
                     Alex loved shells and driftwood
and is dead, a lone gardener, and I
am sitting in Shinjuku, in Tokyo, thinking it over.

Post Card, Moss Garden

This might have been where Lady
Murasaki read

advantaged exile down from
court, "over the hill"

yet beautiful, read and read
and then lay buried.

Over these hills of moss lies
the age of Thirty

a tall white wall surmounted
by tiles incised "yin

yang" and by, beyond, green trees
waxing coherent

in blue skies, no obstacles.
You see distances

closely. Farther over land
than water. No obstacles.

Student Letter

After the declaration by emperor
to stop the war
many people in Tokyo killed themselves,
for instance, in front of the imperial palace.
But few people knows those facts.

Hence you must teach me
where you got the news or what sort of book
gave you the fact that quite few people knows.
To know the fact of our nation's subjection
is not so comfortable
but the fact of many people's spontaneous death
gives me more complicated feelings.

In the matter of what William Gass said
I must describe my feelings. I went
to Nagasaki
on an educational trip four years ago.
I can recollect those serious moment
which was given by the beamed materials
in the memorial hall.

But most youth after the war
are indifferent to those
nightmares
because of our no experience. Surely,
I think, those barbarious conducts
shouldn't be forgiven or forgotten at all
and we must not close our eyes
to the rebombing
at any place
in this world.

In conclusion I may say that most people
except sufferers
or the like
will not have ill feelings toward your country
but they will reproach
the suffocative fact
in history.

Where were you when the World War II was over.
Please share your experience of the war with me.
I'm now interested in the wars concerned with Japan
for the past 100 years. If you tell me your reflections
I can suspect more seriously.
You have abandoned such cursed things as useless?
In that war 3 million people were killed
on the side of our nation, especially
three hundred thousand people by the A-bomb.
Over the war between the imperialism
and militarism America won a victory.
What does this word mean?

Charley

Minnesota, May 1945
DMZ, September 1967

1

In Tokyo our gallant boys
dance rock-and-roll, squint eyes
wary at standing easy. They leer and reel
on a springboard tip and then
jackknife toward the electronic noise . . .

And Charley, when Time Inc. said he said
the President had his head
wedged about Vietnam,
        burning for honor or—who knows?
the Action he had said—
        married the Marines.
He showered vows on those

who took his word who taught him
shoot it out and shout "Yes Sir Yes Sir!"
        and sent him out like napalm
obedient to any itchy finger.

I hope the fields of Minnesota gave perspective
when he moved out
           as to the starting line
on the command, *survive, survive*.

. . . our juiced doughboys feel their girls.

2

    What
did I tell you

when we met
last and it

"after the leeches and the food"
on a break
            in the rain
was already up with you, Charley?

Mouthing the big cigar
like a gangster at the wheel . . .

            cigarette between thumb and finger
            the way we all even in junior high
            learned not to
            your men watching in wonder

            him tasting the strange
                  (turned officer so young)
            foreign taste
            that smoke: and all was dark
                  except what sparks
            he scattered there, stubbing it out

What could we do for you

you hugging your knees

            who taught you
            to raise your voice?

            3

No more the wide Mankato pearled with ice
            under blue January sky
your arm around the shoulder of the friend who ran faster
no more the long hours pad in hand composing

       reasons for your belief
a belief in fathers has no reason

no more the simple passion of going first
your hatless straightness, the struggle, the deep worry,
       the dark Africa of being alive in a country
       run by chiefs without tribes
no more of all that, only your
       brief beauty in many hearts
in a time when fathers bury their sons, and you
       surrounded, cut down
in a war you were fated never to see,
       blinded by love for all men.

Moving Out

You never know to what your knowing tends,
you know as the soldier knows what he must do
and move uncertainly to certain ends.

And at midnight what the turn you turn portends
in the dense alerted woods is lost from view.
You never know to what your knowing tends

and don't know what it is gives way, what bends,
when you writhe through passions you by chance pursue
and move uncertainly to certain ends

and fail to tell which shapes are your few friends
through all the benighted, ready retinue.
You never know to what your knowing tends

as the soldier does not know what he defends
when he moves out, nor does he wish to know,
and moves uncertainly to certain ends;

you lose the thread on which your life depends
and never hear the shot that rips you through;
you never know to what your knowing tends
and move uncertainly to certain ends.

Suburb

Are the rats little
Buddhas? Poisoned by the old
lady upstairs they
do not know it yet. And look
with their usual
cynical sweetness at us
from the kitchen floor.
Their tails still brush our *shoji*
at night. They still play.
They get used to everything.
The style of dying. Of us.

Shore

The stormbird
out, overhead,
circles in darkness. His ring
is inferred.

Up somewhere
out ahead
or behind this spit, lies his aim,
his need.

And gulls strain
on the sea-groin,
adze trawling their cries between stars
and white foam.

Their lone song
does, does belong
on this delta of the dark world.
All, they ring

out, they roam
pluming the stream
of wind, dervish of storm, shriven
of sensed doom.

I would know
how well they do
in the wheels they ride and the posts they keep,
here below.

From the Fastest Train

Kyoto/Tokyo

Each field is gone again

freak snow erasing boundaries
and still the same as yesterday
save a few edges softened here and there . . .

What is their endeavor that
helmeted argonauts
burning for days through frost-paned space
seek keener distances than these
to speculate upon?

After the smogged capital
to see the splendor that earth
snowbound
sunbound conveys

dazzling on the morrow when snows
sealed by night truck ruts, work track, ditch
and haystack
burn in the sun

giving the land seamless
identity, time with space, imagine
heaven that state
of final assurance locked in a trance of light like this
lone farmer carrying sticks of fuel
down snow drift toward his gate.

And
in a bright bay of space
rides the black ship of Schoolmen's sons
from which glassy astronauts
all weightless and aware

plunge spacecraft snowshoes down
to tiptoe
seedless fields, quicksand dust,

quicksilver the cloudless day
that recedes always before them
into the black sun strewn everywhere . . .

is it undisguised
erotic sighs
          or just some
mild grief, "wild surmise"
when these brief desperadoes of themselves

look up from sandwiches and watch their world
an opened orange on the shore of night?

Black speck caught in sheeted amber

the farmer cared always
never to answer
          bends to mend his gate
into the sun strewn everywhere
micas of Kansai noon lodged

in the warm blood of
          work to do
gate hinges rusty   blood
in fingers numb red bands
in agate, gristle
and broken bolt:
         to be done
—begun before
knowledge and not ever

       done.

FROM
Riding to Greylock (1983)

End of the Picaro

The path strewn with leaves, lined with kempt bushes
Behind which someone languished for salvation

The path that trailed off in the confining
Attenuations of perspective (which alone
Seemed to beckon and comfort) the wanderer
Before a cut stone wall stalled in wonder

Where in the stones were hewn fragments of letters
QR, VT, and so forth: so that even
A picaro soon saw what he had come to

The something larger he'd been thrown up out of
As these remains of masonry still grander—
Edifice once of stunning proportions—decked
With mottos of obedience, loyalty, pomp:
But now the lesser from the greater ruin.
Some eighteen feet or more where tendrils grip
The scattered letters broken to unbreakable
Code. The trail stops here.
                    Or here. And here.
Or so: it merely fails in brakes where kudzu
Wild grape and raspberry lashes rope and knot.

In much the same way your knack of finding
                    in the picaro what you desire:
To have his scrapes
His trips & happy tangos with relenting ogres
Means what you desire because to begin with
You sent him forth. You never had to open a book
And always he smiled over his shoulder
The musket propped against a birch while he
Laced up his buskins, Gil smiled forever
At you following
                    Letting you know he knew:
A genie of daydreams, loyal, obedient, true.

His fealty was the important part
And no converging symmetrical plot imposed
            by an author who
In his closet wisdom
Made plot subserve your quest. But you, the you
Shackled within
                who would pay out, be picaro
Never content to play some anecdotal bit
Part in the corporate folly history,
Venerable rosary. Here your youth
Stymied at the stricken plot of the world
Stands at the edifice eternity
Defaces and like an Asian god, with eyes
Averted, effaces himself and doubles back
And homeward, down tangled banks, to your first need.

At Peaks Island

There on the tangle of granite planes
And mica glintings, on the torn
Wrappings of sunlight and a cord of crystal
Tying an edge, someone had left
Beside a patch of lichen and a square of moss

A box of Binney & Smith Crayola crayons, *carnation*
Pink, sea green, periwinkle, burnt sienna
Half a *maize*, a stub of *sky*
Blue. They looked
Ready to use again
After a musing child had colored in a lichen
Or dotted the nightshade with purple dots;
The box of colors seemed to lie there ready
To turn a pebble red or blue, to heighten a petal: but not

To spray "Lucy Grillo Loves George Rockwood"
In dumb letters on the face of the concrete
Bunker down the shore, this dated rockery
For men to spot the Nazi U-boats from;

And least of all to be taken up
To draw the seascape, stubs too blunt
For noon, for a horizon, or
The join of plane and fracture.
(I took them, I tried to capture
Those minimal, burning edges
Of magnitude. The page became
A jam of trails blindly grappling
Unending volumes, as warped with accident
As a child's map of seeing.)

*

Summer people here
Gather along the shore road at sunset
Or wade in Spar Cove
And know where not to hang their monickers: not
On the scoured knee of a rawboned sea cliff, not to color
The unknown, reserving their penchant to say
"Bernie Loves Minta" for the bunkers they know
Where uncles waited for years at the ready
With radios, Spam, the letters from home, the blankets
Lining each olive-drab nest

And watched the convoys from Portland gliding
To the contested seas, guarded by these
Concrete towers, dazed with amnesia now, long-haired
Stone faces under sumac and beach grass;
Or the warren of deep-tunneled loggias for guns
Below. There my desire
To wander knew no end. There
The shadows cling, damp with old toil,
Secrecy, absence. Anonymous, empty gun-bays
Receive a spray of naming now, "Civitarese
& Conkey," "Robin Rottin Crotch," and even
"Mein Fraülein ist auch shön."

I turned to you once, standing alone
On a parapet frowsy with daisies
While the last islanders sauntered toward their porches.
The outline of your peaceful shoulders, scintillant
In a fine dust of light from the banked sun rippling,
Burning westward over the rim of mainland.
(I took the *red violet*,
I drew it up my shin along the bone
And then with the piece of *nasturtium gold*
I wrote your name across my thigh.)

Flight of Steps

Though [La Pietra] had been bruised and abandoned, the garden had assumed a patina as of antique bronze, as if it had been standing on the hillside since the seventeenth century . . . This was the background of my boyhood and we had grown up together . . . weeds burst through the cracks and forced their way through the pebble-patterned stairways; the stone vases were empty, the gates were coated with rust . . . I could not see it again with the innocent eyes of my youth but the thoughts and emotions long dormant came drifting back.

—Sir Harold Acton

1

Farewell, then, to this
    Residue of place, their styled
Concessions dapper
    With tattersall and webbing
Lounges; the kiosk
    Of junk! The folks smile on; they
Quaff tall drinks on their
    Decks imbrued with creosote
Bossed with loud statues
    And raw-glass insulators.

For aftermath, the catatonic apartment.
    In the roominghouse yard a scrap of snow in mud.
A bare arm hanging out a window, or one
    Dirty big toe, cold at the mouth of a broken
Shoe. Budweiser cans, three grapefruit skulls under the
    Window of the girl painter.

2

On the edge, having
    About had it, he cried, "I
Might have given out
    Life, or the slice I cherished

To *Progress.*" And now
          Even as he is about
To be left alone
          He wants this: to lose his place.

You laughed, and the match
          For your smoke went out once more.
Laughing was over-
          Flow. It parleyed with the flame
          Saying, "I'll make the flame here."

          3

          Look here: his black tracks
Grow larger, swell as snow melts
          —Frankenstein trekking
North. Yard-long boot shapes pool, merge
          With the salty Interstate.

          Lithe hours havoc
And absorb each drift; footprints
          Vanish into each
Other. Remember the rings,
          Grass around tree trunks
Come spring, pressing out as if
          To settle summer's
Limit of shade? Direction
          Erases itself.
Perspectives extend. A time
          Destructs, flame blown to zero.

          4

He never thought this raging furnace of the head
          Would get him beyond
And yet he did. He mumbled, or considered how
          All wordings of it scrambled.

When you wrote under
    Maples at a worn picnic
Table you found one
    Knothole, knot long gone, plugged now
    By paper, marked with faint words.

     5

The clouds like Indians
    On snowshoes with bowstrings taut
Absorb the traces,
    Pick off great destinies. He
Might make himself scarce
    Now, smooth over his brushstrokes,
Try for an exact
    Anonymous mid-distance.

After Sunday's frost
    Under the white pines, a fresh
Carpet of needles
    Dry, smooth, slippery. He slides,
Leather soles skate over them.

     6

    A kind of peace spilled
    As if everything that he
Counted on had split
    Underground, the good pictures
The fair legs, the gifts
    (Not overwhelming perhaps
But choice) survivals
    From a terrace more ample
With lemons and box
    Hedges among these mellow
    Cinders of his lot, gifts—not
Memories quite—that

Had been a matter of life
Bequeathing him hope
    Through the salvos of wise smiles
    And the shined quarters of prose.

7

    Through fur-twigged sumac
One jay rules. Jay, jay, brainy
    Bird, you hammer out
Your protocols unheard. One
    Jag of blue against
Greens; loud at strewn umbers, at
    Rifle green, greens deeper still!

Some Flowers

Lilacs flower by old roads
And purple loosestrife in marshes by the sea
Cool beads of sweat
Bloom on the glass that brims with vin rosé
And carries in its bowl
One little flower of the sun

While shots from rooftops crack out mocking
And flames bloom
Out from tenements, long tiger
Lilies, Shiva's arms
Slow cobras in the swirl of fire
We carry one another
House to house

And room to room
Nerves unmotored by forbidden flowers

This friend too burned to hold a water glass
And when we lift him from the couch
We feel the heft of knowledge we may not hold on to
Something that is earthly, heavy
In our bodies alone

Or later mornings
When the moist street gives back
A golden litter from the sun
We plunge ahead, as the light
Changes, against ourselves.

In the Dakotas

The head of a fence post glances
Splintering in the sun.
A season; wooly bears creep west,
They vanish with his wheels.

A winded rose lies torn from the wall,
Mist trails from the pine lot
Where he, departing, calls
Mother, calling her one name,

A whole grammar of longing
Where cowled autumns hover.
The wet macadams, iridescent,
Give back smears of light

Blueprints of
Spring's butterflies.

Tom and Henry, Camping Out

Well, Ford, people like us, we
Don't have to worry. We have the river
Coming up just here. Dancing came

Naturally, easy as misprint in a bunch
Of kids setting their own type. We had
Palazzo font, and the right note

Of resignation. To find purple gauze
Or gold faience on morning coffee means
The whole day will go by like a nap.

We had the cherry flowering above us
Where we lounged like arrived mallards
The voluble petals billowing

Around us whispering, "How far is down?"
We had a candle ready and watched the lightning
Shred up from the landing field in the valley

When the transformer went. You laughed,
"Never explain." We knew if we could step out
Of our bodies they would fill up with those garnets.

Mithuna

They were
cedar waxwings side
by side, helmeted;
two sparrows (English)
in mufti
elm by
elm, mute snow coasting;
cardinals clearing
for winter; or one
pair crows in clean kit:
never on a branch
together attend
each other.
The fanned
feathers of the tail
hold down aft the bark
where twig hands sternly
prehensile argue
the cowled weathers for
judgments of balance.

So the wall-eyed stares
offer in answer
steady pulls
and tail
feathers, opposed con-
cerns, peg in space those
tents of their bodies.
Even with such trained
severe responses
always when one bird
watches its mate or
(merely) another

the second cannot
return the regard
received, unable

to acknowledge such
communion of air:
but watches, watched, sway-
ing with the mast of
the tree, focuses
(as if so much was
worth his life) with a
sensible bead on
a thorn or mote in
the thicket of air,
a spore of deer moss
or the green aphid
of a rose.

Nativity

Only husbands wearing gowns
permitted beyond this point
—Maternity ward sign

A picture-windowed fifth-floor room:
above the rubble of delivery tables
the rubber sheets and terry towels
tray and stirrup, clamp and bolt,
a kind contraption shows the portal of your womb.
Among the arc lights everywhere
a convex mirror hung
above us like a shield
mediates, enlarging this far-flung
spectacle. May we not miss
the moment, paradise
of generation verified; *now* made minutely visible!

From slippery boards where we had danced
cobwebbed performers growing old
two seniors of Shalott feeling the cold
together we observed right breathing through the fast.
Suddenly lost
finding your own, as in a dream, you cry at last.
Dumbfounded spirits then, entranced
and hand in hand, a doubled Perseus,
behold this stun-
ning end of one.
The mirror returns
its image of
one love
becoming two; the utterly sumptuous
revolt.

You watch Medusa slowly wakening from sleep to flood
this gate of bone shifting to yawn in larger
gapes of you; and soon

the crown, like a shadow moon
through mist, appears
ghostly lanugo and bone, the chromium charger
with clamps like fangs, drenched hair
and plume of blood
and how you lost
—cried *No!*, your fare-thee-well to years
when the last great Hokusai wave, towering, tossed
you back, combed through us there
with rifling fold
furling along that shore
of incandescent light.
With distance doubled by the brilliant shield
we watch it yield
no stone, no harm, but suffered bliss.
Hard looking has afforded this.

The dazzled retina, then the Persian blue
sky I saw that shone above your head.
Stars and planets gleamed, spun
in one
boreal candelabrum,
shone out far from the saddle and the sheet
lighting a way, this exile from
ourselves, this passing through.

When all was done
twin cries declared what had begun:
your own, and this anomalous squinting incubus
a magnum of champagne uncorked
such great nothings-to-do-with-us!
Forgotten now in that hospitable tumult
we were begotten too. Henceforward forked:
pinned on our astonished tines;
that business, this result:
one sociable camp meeting

or stairway of a summer night—
and now, surprised by her small muscular hellos
we greet our own charisma, anodyne;
three rare birds flushed to flight
under one sign.

A Little Yard

Sunlight hugs the walls.
The house is ticking. Winter's
Cardiac arrest.

Spring now; you can read
In the garden. Then you use
One sock for bookmark.

From the stump of the
Old willow, shoots arch, saffron
Stem and leaf. Clare, just
Two, sits there in shade, hands in
Her lap. "What Clare do!" she cries.

The bumblebee scouts
Me; moves on. I rest now, no
Flower after all.

You disappear then
To leave just us together.
The violets you
Were picking lie on the walk
Strewn from here to the back door.

Clare mounts the picnic
Table, sprawls on the warm height;
Copying the cat.

Condensation

A wisp of straw hangs from
      The apple branch. On his window
Condensation blurs his
      View; couples walking by the
      River. Apples, spilled by a wall.

This autumn plenty. There,
      White noise from the heart. And no one
To hear the old voices,
      The singing. The cricket critches
      Moonward from the cooling hearth. This

Small clamor in his blood
      Is somehow some small knowledge of
His child: which will become
      A protean encroachment on
      The petty dark of solitude.

Possession is nine-tenths
      Of the disenchantment. The hills
Go platinum with frost.
      He could remember keeping score,
      All those infatuations in the wind.

Then letting it go. And
      Letting go, he let time alone.
Only the breezy young
      Have nothing in common, though
      They share findings. They find common

Cause against calendars
      And fear another hand on the
Misted pane where, smiling,
      A girl peers in on them, a gold
      Leaf in her damp, night-tangled hair.

Survivor, Walking

Malcolm Cowley

He knew the stories he could tell
    Like his own garden—well.
And then he knew the woods, could tame
    Each wildness with a name.
    Fondly he rapped the knees
    Of ancient, familiar trees

With his green beechwood hiking staff.
    Their silence swelled his laugh
As he saluted those careers
    He'd followed forty years.
    Half rot, half youthful still,
    Growth was their only skill.

"Across this trunk note how the sun
    Shows burnished cinnamon."
(His loud, half-deaf discourse.) "The bark
    No longer looks just dark,
    It lives a hundred years
    Or so, till this appears."

Growling in anger once, he stopped
    Before some spruces lopped
(Years back) at the neck for Christmas trees.
    He cried, "Now look at these
    Some bastard has got at!
    Who'd do a thing like that?"

One birch, in a woodlot maples won,
    Leaned there, a veteran
Stripped naked, where its sun had failed.
    Even this one he hailed
    Like an impoverished friend
    Remembered to the end.

At home, on trees pulped down, he wrote
　　Critique and anecdote.
Working out front, working backstage
　　He chronicled his age
　　And by this balanced act
　　Delivered up the fact.

On walks he still hails trees recalled
　　By name, or stops, enthralled
By one no logger has cut down
　　And lightning missed, whose crown
　　Rails yet against the sky,
　　Still at it, green and spry.

He will not hear us, not by half.
　　Silences make him laugh.
Beyond our powers to persuade
　　He drops his hearing aid
　　And marches to the woods
　　To join his earthly goods.

Prefect

Windrose
of upland clearing

lichened outcrop
each crevice

bubbling moss
milk quartz—

notched granite
nudging sheep—

cropped grass
coppery

tip of earthcrust
dry rose

petals sailing
volumes of lean

Pleistocene air
comb turf, the blue

juniper tongues
all one way

I the other
look back,

perfect
stranger.

Northway Tanka

White leaves, magenta
Leaves, curled in grass. A brown mesh
Of needles, freshly
Spread. One opened husk, the nut
Tucked safe in a secret place.

*

Sun struts from cloud then:
Now mica stars stream past, make
Macadam twinkle
Racing under, around me;
Mighty pines of night, each side.

*

Over the cleared fields
Striding and mountain shadows
Stream, draining earth's warmth.
Outside, a dog whines.
A clear sky, cleared for winter.

*

Black spaces under pines.
Ahead, a vast cold front, cloud
Range level, half to
Zenith: a wall of winter
At the far end of the world.

*

Blind as pain these men
Stand, stretching by their parked cars.
Hoods shine apart where
Beyond mountains swim into
The great mandala of light.

*

Dolorous granite
Rock like a crouching lion,

Tumbled by glaciers!
Rock like a crouching lion
Rock like a crouching lion!

*

A shred of cloud trails
The mountain face; catches
On a pine: below
A striped lump that is, that was
Raccoon; and one Piels beer can.

*

Lifted from its bed
By a passing wind the leaf
Raised the brown profile
Of a chipmunk. Then it sank
Back; but stood again; again.

*

To stand in a field
Silenced and drained for winter
Where one clover blooms
And hear, muffled by distance,
The geese calling for summer!

Ribboning silence
They keep forming, keep a long
Communal mewing.
I stood there when I heard this
Wan assumption of their cries.

*

The two-rut dirt road
Trailed from the four-lane highway
Dissolving shortly
In dense toils, second-growth scrub.
My country, O my country!

When it was summer
The long rain fell silently
Soaking grass and earth:
Now on beds of brittle leaves
Cold rains tattoo ceaselessly.

Still in place the leaves
Of a poplar, lime and gray,
Simmer together
On the wind. A squall flaps them,
The words blow off my page.

I walk these dry paths
Under bare branch and bare sky.
Through the leaves' ruin,
Churning loudly, my feet go.
With snow, this too will be stilled.

When I drove southward
Through trees ranked on a ridge crest
The sun, setting, west,
Paced me: a rapid fire
Stuttered between trunks stock still.

Declension

In the chorus of memories a blessing in disguise.
The birds and the trees are satisfied. If these
Appear to grow smaller with distance how
Tell of the particulate the towering
Matter of the pine, its needles, or its osprey
Waiting magnanimous upon the sun
You saw from the curl of the bend back-rising there?

The tree, its mossed feet, the mane green:
Manor for whom, for what? The bird, or song
You had to ignore, heading on. A death?
Not knowing, you ignored the tree, the osprey.
What is not yours is that beyond the time
You do; or might be; or, "Once upon a time . . ."

Spare, untouchable, the river bank. And there
White water, phrasing, racing past you, back.
Particular roadside pines, converging walls
Backing the head—to vanishing point. A sense
Of acrid pine musk that might have been there lingers,
Remembered. The graceful ornaments linger on
And overwhelm.
                    How then will you get on
To what you know, as you must? The eggshell
On the garden path; the tanager's intent
In tapering branches? All this is what is not
For you, and the words rise outward to your smile.

Oyster Cove

The macadam is flaking and the lilac
Too big to bloom
Fingers a cobweb of smoky light from the terrace,
Grazes the sun-chalked cedarshakes. And no surprise.

Gone the lady, to Athens or Anjou. Her sunroom
Oozes silence. The paisley over the back
Of a wicker rocker. The pedals of her grand hover
Above the calm sea of the tiled floor

Like gilt clouds, each brazen ball
Without a claw. In Roseville jardinieres
Iron geraniums stiffen and chip;
A noose of rose and the scum of ferrous

Oxide throttle the sundial's Horatian tip
For those noddy panamas and white-ducks of class.
In the pergola woodflies on the pedestal
Walk all over it. What are years?

Or at the stoned gazing globe's crashed glass
Peek in on themselves, magnified; what's more,
Behold no Chloe nor her golfing lover
In the mullioned saucers of their eyes.

Balance

Through the yellow leaves you go,
Alert to the three acres
Around you, and remember
All that you knew about
Hunting with bow and arrow.
You scan the woods for miles

For hours peaceful as Quakers.
Birches, like falling snow
In sunlight, blur. You hear
A squirrel or a finch.
Take aim. At last the bowstring
Cracks, loud. A deer flings

His half-acknowledging
Stare back at you. The last
Thing you learned: sit down,
One hour. How many spikes
Were there? He's ambled off!
A careful arrow strikes

Flank or hindquarter so
Lightly (though it will take
Hold, work deep) at first
The deer fails to notice
And flicks as if to shake
A fly off, or at worst

Shies back some yards; and goes
On grazing. Your presence must
Be known, if you begin
To track at once. Your quarry—
If you so much as flinch—
Takes flight; adrenalin

Will keep him up for miles.
If you have taken trust
From the October light
He'll find the time and wiles
To lose you, as he loses
Blood. But don't alarm him

And blood will slowly clot,
Slowly he will weaken
And quietly lie down
And, as the blood cools, find
He's rooted to the spot
Where he caught sight of you.

He will die there near you
Where with silent presence
You sat through it all
And did not move an inch,
Holding the animal
And your deed in level balance.

The Austin Tower

Charles Whitman, Texas, 1966

If I talked with you tomorrow.
But
    I have cut off my ear
My treasured lobe

No one will know

I cannot hear you anymore
In this
Music about music about music.

I have
Turned in all
My cards. There is

Too much organ music
In my ear.

*

I came out of the rain, the train had stopped
The glass buildings spurted corn silk from rooftops
It was afternoon, I decided: *not in uniform.*
The city came up fast the din
Fell around like snow. The blizzard of

My sunlight. I spent a third of my life
Wearing my radio, wearing
My weaponry, gaining and
Losing.
There are stretch marks on my heart.

What empty vessels
Achievement patches from eagles
The barbecues of fighting or fitting
In, frail silks, nauseous, jockeying for wins
The red wins, long weeks learning to swim
With grace to shiver at their dock.

*

This life is bluegrass, turn it up
I love you all, but

I am uncharitable. I
                    have
No love for you.

I am here, on this porch.
        The radio is plastic.
There is a plastic kazoo
There is
A shiny Lawson gutbucket.
The singer has a tiki round his neck
But he does not really come from California

There is music.
There was.
We have cut off our ears.
        My
Fucking father!
The door is open

Nobody is afraid of the razor strop
Hanging, the nail in the closet
The braid rug on the wall.
It makes me

I cannot
Make out the way and is it
                    Trembling or
                    Just fumbling I have to know
These feelings are an arbitrary pack
Trussed in a town I never lived in

                    My body
Hangs around me
Like a street gang round a yokel from upstate
                    Each move I make
Flips back, I wince

Then I get tired
Getting around—from check to check—
I am in a car without lights at night
                    In an open field
                    Seeking the road.

          When she turned aside
          From coffee and went down
                    Inside, to get the train
                    Inside the black street

          When you turned aside
          And sliced your wrists like celery sticks
                    They turned you out
                    Into a white room

          I lost thirty pounds
          The need of talking went; the idea of food
                    I thinned out
                    Around my navel and my mouth

They said I looked younger
I was the well-kept place in a suburb
    What grew that no one cared for
    Thinned out, trimmed back, pruned.

                    *

Under the searchlight of the sun
Full volume

I've got the Black station

    All the keys they have given my life
    To open and close the doors which held me
    Open and close the rooms that clothed me
    Enter enter and enter the cells of bank accounts
    The manual of arms performed each night

    To please him
    To start up the cancer machine
    To walk the straight hall of impotence, keys
    Of warm beds sprinkled with old china broken
    Warm beds sprinkled with oiled steel, the M-1, in bits
    This is my weapon, this is my gun
    This is my weapon, this is my gun
    Lockers loaded with jockstraps and Egyptian unguents
    Immense combinations which opened stars

I look in the mirror and get the "exact change"
I look in the mirror, which doubles distances
I have grown
Smaller and smaller, my mouth is a hole
My lips were taken long ago
For eyes they have fitted in balls of Syrian glass
That peer through slits in pillows the phlegm makes
Plumbing up from the swollen bags of sinuses
My nose is a cherry, it has dipped in many mugs
And there are stretch marks on my belly

Like vapor trails in a sunless sky
Out from the dead mouth of my navel.

This is the way I love myself
This is the naked body in the mirror.
Father! I am burned again
My ambition will not
Consume me. No
All it is
Is you go out and get hooked once more

The wafer dry-sealed on the roof of my mouth.

    Rare bird the size of a pea
    Up on the tower in Austin
    To those of you
    Below strolling into

    These human arms.

Nothing, Nothing at All

To be the diamond on the hilt of a sword
I have at length misplaced beyond recall;
To feel no more, because I am loved enough
And I return as much: like letters of credit

This joy entitles me; like a license to vend
Dark wines. To his beloved, man is a rainbow
Visible only from the other side
Of the weather of which he is the sign,

Of the sun of which he is reflection.
You see you are the poem you disregard,
You see that what you have not given up
At last not even memory could hold.

All that remains to be relinquished now
Is what you always held out for, this desire
To be desired, which keeps and tops the rim
Of any wellhead you had ever prized.

Bridge of Abandonment

Anne Sexton

The door was painted on the wall

In your room you worked
The filing cabinet
Mining the load
Of memorabilia

Your Death, dressed like the Good Gray Poet
Still leaned over your shoulder
Biting your neck
Leaving a brown-out hickey, token
Of ashen skylines
The seven bridges of a sexy life
Black moon blazoning a white shield

Still somewhere up the heart
There'd be another year for crooning
In spite of the zeroes of monoxide

Clear water in cold light
Treading old rocks that make
Strong water hardly ripple
Brim or curl

Made a thing to wonder at

Black door, white wall.

The Last of the Wallendas

             Another night, the dapper
        Anthology of stars lights up.
The constellations, those jam pots
        The young in their political beards
                Raise gymnast pyramids toward.

                        *

By Saturday at two the ancient allegiances
        The stroked and the unstroked
                Called out to remind us

Of a bronze-age glade
        Where even the stuffed toys
                Were fitted out by Puvis de Chavannes.

                        *

        Holding your arms in mine
        One weight describing
        The brother arc
        From balance to balance,
        Or back to back
        To breathe, filling each other through
        Solder of sweat
        With arms outstretched we took
        The lash of applause from the dark
        Pit below. You spoke
        Joy to have no guard to have
        The courage to enact it

        Not just talk about it.
        It is I who have been unlike you
        Dreaming hard
        When searchlights singled us
        Wired for thrills
        As if we were an enemy
        Within their wall.
        Our act is finished.

Who was I
To you but your loss
Your twin
The ground you gave?

*

Listen; the stone in the mill is grunting,
The voice from the river calls still.
In your own smile smiled over
Your own bounds
Was the suture that held.

*

High between
Two buildings
The old man, blue
As a Chagall angel,
Is falling
The outline of
His body so small

Like an ankh
And the open mouth
Grinning or
Crying out,
"How I wanted you
Boys to know
I believed
The lines of my life."

FROM
Man in the Open Air (1988)

Letter from Stony Creek

Ground zero all at once; after rain, this brightness.
The hollow sea grass hummocks thump when I
Jump down, or kneel to gather glasswort, red
And cold. Blue juniper, rose hip, towering reed
Plume in eyes, ears, nose, here at the quarry,
Crater of water mantled with green and one duck;
Granite cubes long gone to the Statue of Liberty.
Behind, the Sound gleams on Mr. Kingsley's cottage,
Light off the water ablaze on the twill of slates.
Slimmed by the sun behind her, a woman is riding
Her bicycle on the pier. See, she is on the waves!
I want you to picture the cars in line to the city,
To Monday; now, the obvious ease of all, if only
For a moment. Experience itself is a cul de sac.
Depths in the rock beckon. Lichens peel, and you
See in. The light on the water trembles; rises.

Ray's Garden Shop

Bony Ray Plummet
at the end of Center Road
    on the Hoosac shore

among the willows
around his lean-to raised plants
    and vegetables

junipers, vinca
(and other ground covers) a
    "specialty," which he

sold from his dooryard
to local farmers and such
    as found the dirt road.

A modest living,
Ray in his *Hood's Milk* warm-up
    jacket would say; you

won't believe it, friend,
I'm in retirement here.
    In pink on blue boards

he was daubing signs
about his sturdy myrtle,
    his delphinium,

squatting in the dust
which spread over his lean arms,
    his seedlings and his

long array of signs
announcing the quality
    of his flowers, more

bountiful words and
more colors than his flowers.
    He stood to shake hands

warming to the chance
visitor, making ready
    to chat his ear off.

Winters this place gets
too cold, so I take off; drive
    down to Florida:

he pointed to his
sedan, half garaged and half
    disguised with creeper.

How odd it was, but
we must pass the time of day
    If I did not buy

or if I did. He
was too cheerful and too weird
    for me. I was hot

to get out of there,
when his hand gripped my elbow.
    He dropped to his knees

and said, I don't know
what your beliefs are, I don't
    want to offend you

but I believe that
heaven and hell are right here
    on this earth. Mind you

I'm no *atheist*
but, see, after flesh-and-blood
     it's bye-bye baby.

Incidentally,
friend, just look, this marvelous
     stuff growing away

right on the shoulder
right in the oil and sand and all
     this dust. He bent his

old dry body down
and held a head of dust-white
     hen-and-chickens for

me to see. This here
is it, he said. I gave him
     a hand and he stood.

You're kidding me now,
I said. We grinned and hugged while
     a car, as surely

as the dawning of
manly knowledge in a boy,
     came on, down the slow

road, a leading edge
trailing a fresh plume of dust
     toward Plummet's garden,

like the shadow of
a cloud moving overhead
across the sun and

drawing a dark squall
over the bowed grass, the white
and shivering leaves.

The Heart's Desire of Americans

Squally Election Day, a few drops pebbling
The hood; we wanted a bite to eat but wanted
To vote, to get back to vote; although not voting
Counted, too. We turned in the drive of Concord
Prison, backtracked through drizzle and at the sign
For Walden Pond turned off, on impulse to pay
A visit; parked where a crowd in cars sat talking
In the rain or silently watching it spatter the pond.
Tuesday: they should have been at work. But clearly
They had the day off to vote; and here they were.
Walden, we guessed, had been a glacial kettle
Or the like; since the wooded banks were steep, no way
For the water to get in or out that we could see.
There was a concrete pier with ladders and a beach,
A woman's bath house and a men's, and signs that said
"No Swimming." The rain on the wooden trails was beautiful.

*

Jim said, "I believe everything you say,"
Which made me feel good although I knew of course
There was more than a touch of irony in his voice
And the way he laughed I knew he doubted me
When I told him the last words of Thoreau, as who
Wouldn't. We split a granola bar and decided
To make up proverbs. "He who looks for dustballs
Under the bed is not looking" seemed the most
Likely, here. Goofer feathers, dust puppies, and
Angel fluff we acknowledged as acceptable
Variant wordings for this Concord saw.
We wanted to look, but the rain was not letting up
And still we could not go for coffee without
First changing the old, frayed windshield wipers
For new ones, which he had thoughtfully brought with him,
Some "fits all" kind, not simple to attach at all.

*

Slant capes of rain spilled down and fled, scoring
The dark waters till Walden simmered with light,
While more people arrived in sparkling cars.
Two women in running suits had remembered to bring
A flowered parasol and plain umbrella, which
They put up as they sauntered down the path
Of white pine needles toward the shore. We decided
Not to waste our time, and be on our way. "Zen mind,
Weekender's mind," Jim said, and so it seemed.
It was a beautiful time. Even the prison looked
Empty, and the girl at the ice cream counter smiled.
Later, the Deerfield River and its arrangement
Of ice-planed rocks streaming with rain and the late
Twilight gleaming beside Route Two urged us
To stop. And we pulled over. When you've seen
One perfect spot, you want to see them all.

Egyptian Onions

Athwart, nudging each other,
The fat Egyptian onions teeter
As if they were dozing on guard
In the garden of Ceres; stiffen
And pale, contending with aster
And ragweed, each plump column
Flaring, bowed with the weight
Of its berry-bunch capital; a little temple
Sprouting the ruin of itself.

Blisters of tiny onions, bitter
Lilies, nod to the wind,
White wisps of minuscule root hairs
Curling in the afternoon air
Like the thinnest beard of the wisest sage,
Like the vestige of yearning for darkness,
Loose skeins trolling the air
That yet might fall
To the fuming soil; and drink; and begin.

Command Performance

R.T.S.L.

There was no mound to mark your burial
When the Russian poet wandered there,
Backing away to gaze at the flame sky.

The tears you blinked back filled your eyes
The day we came to cheer you up.
You lay across that bed like a manatee

Cocky as Long John Silver bluffing,
Jawing to Kathy, pale from miscarriage, and to me
Of Allen's twins,

How a son had strangled. Then
Laughing and coughing you
Set course for Quincy's guest suite bathroom,

Your chin crooking as if to hold a violin.
Uncrowned, unvanquished
Your landed mind held court.

Your loving friends took care always,
Fanny and Grey, Bingo, Elizabeth, Bill
Though you are gone still willing

To lend the hand you never could take.
The river by Dunbarton flows
Seaward, luminous, calm in its wide banks,

Steady into the growing dark
Where the Russian poet your friend
Friend only of your poems now

Ponders the stones and the chance flower,
Backing away to the city, to the perilous
Passions of those you commanded to love.

The White Oak of Eagle Bridge

Below the house it reached its black arms across the sky.
Those arms spread—you might think if you stood under them—
Horizon to horizon; at least from the peak of my roof
To the milk shed across the road. There I stood and watched
From its long veranda of shade my field over the road
Being mown and raked. One year I went to lend a hand,
The summer Joseph's rake broke down, the sheaves gathering
Sunlight as they rose to the gray, longsleeved arms
Of Joseph Judd, his collarless cotton shirt buttoned,
Then to the arms of his wife blue-jeaned against hay dust,
Working along with him, Mr. and Mrs. Joseph
Judd the season through like cheerless speechless workers
Of Brueghel, row by row cutting, loading their wagon,
Carrying eight acres of hay in their old arms.

Another year, for taxes, they sold Treddle their mare
For whom they worked the field. No stopping for coffee now,
Courtly half hour in the kitchen when the Judds,
Brushed clean, had done receiving the hay: it had been barter,
I gave good hay for their good work. They stayed at home,
A cape of tarpapered clapboard down by the Hoosac. I watched
The field go white with daisies, yellow with buttercups;
Lavender off to the left, chicory mixing with purple
Clover; mallow, splotches of vetch; soon the popple
Saplings, blinking with light: no good for haying now,
Or not until someone ploughed, if someone wanted to.

One August when the wind leaned on the oak and nudged
The crown an inch or two off plumb, more than was well
With gravity, it leaned and, creaking, leaned more yet as if
Peering over an edge; and fell. I walked, walked
In tears, as if a friend had died. I saw that hollow,
And ants that swarmed sawdust the town crew left behind
When they cleared the road for traffic. So much firewood,
Pitiful sight! Presence of rotting light stormed down
And occupied the whole place: where the burled limbs
Had always made a lichened, shaggy pagoda of tree;

Brackets of lesser branches, bunches of scalloped leaves
That chittered in winter together. An alien light blinded
Thin acidulous grass on the slope, burned out the veins
Five kinds of mushrooms bulged from after a summer shower.

I waited for something to happen, as if one night the tree
Wearing the whole garment of its former harmony
Would return with just the same shock and simplicity
Of its fall, the old dark of its arms webbing the moonlight
That fell on the slope like snow, like the spongy sepulchral
Luminescence of wood rotting.

                                    Another year went by,
The persistence of the oak still made its absence felt
As strongly as when it stood there and made its presence known
On the slope, the benediction of its choosing *here*
To have stayed on, regardless of weathers, not building a name.
As strongly as the absence of Joseph and Mrs. Judd
Who, silently as they worked hayload after hayload,
Had left their river place; bedroom and stable, shed
And parlor, scarved in tar shingle and climbing rose,
Windows boarded, a mullein tall in the dooryard one day
When I walked down to the Hoosac for the great blue herons.
I took the back way home and met my neighbor, Myron,
Still farming at eighty-three and still the town assessor.
We remembered old Joe Judd and Mrs. Judd and wondered
Where they'd gone, and how they lived without this place
And how—for that matter—they had managed with it.
"Judd was always a blank," said Myron, "on our tax roll."
In front of my place now we paused; Myron brought up
That oak. "It had a sickle left hanging in it. Slowly
Swallowed, probably, by the growing. Probably
Still there. Unless the chainsaw came across it and sent it
Flying." And old man Judd, I asked him, what of Judd?
"Well, there's a couple! Don't you worry, they'll do well.
Now your white oak," said Myron, who'd lived the next farm up
Now eighty years, "you know, your white oak stood beside

Another one, exactly like it, girth and crown.
'Twin Oaks' they called your place."

                                    He'd always thought of them
As twins, he said, but saw no point in telling me
A thing from his own childhood when there was only the one
I knew about. I found no trace of the ancient stump;
Myron had forgotten just where that mirror twin,
Invisible perfect tree, had stood, matching what's now
A jagged center where the dark shaft rose beside
The field filling with goldenrod to a man's height;
Popple getting a start; asters; nobody's field.

from Last Days at York Manor

Decoy

With son and father talking, it's no trouble
Killing time. The duck with glass eyes stares,
Shellacked, between them on the carpet; gift
Of old Ted Freeman, who years ago skinned off
The painted feathers (where now we see a great
Lead slug wedged in for ballast) and christened it
A doorstop. Once more he praises me for what
I hardly possess and—out of modesty
Or guilt; or truth—stoutly deny. So why
Are we talking about poetic meter and
Poetic form? Our lives are late for *belles lettres*.
We've known each other forty years and more.
Was it so hard so long to show some life?
But he will inquire again about rhyme scheme,
What rhyme is, honestly now, beyond the sound.
I will respond, rhyme is as when his thought
Resembles a thought his father had, just as
Though my face is mine, all see my father in it.
I might tell him a rhyme is when a man
Becomes a father, but then he'd say something
About a scheme and have me falling silent
And watching my daughter, now playing with the duck.
The mallard's a doorstop, but truly it had been
A decoy, "perhaps a Joe Lincoln," people said,
And had it not been stripped today worth thousands;
Not one of the replicas machines engender.
He quotes me Shakespeare and Sam Pepys; his art
Of conversation highballs past midnight through
The room, the green-eyed mallard on the pond
Of carpet by his grandchild, exhausted girl,
In sleep touching her imagined bird.

Station 41

It is the last stage of day. The bending sky
Streams west; the final peels of peachblow cloud
Drift back. Snowfields below like tarnished brass
Give up a brightness as blues shade them. I
Alone and westward wend behind a crowd
Of men unwinding, each flying business class
With complimentary glass of wine or malt or gin;
After quotidian
Foray, making joyful the noise of return.
I will not see them, grinding at the quern
Of going to the old home, but hear their voices
Like gulls above the stern
Of my ship as it makes for port and the few choices.

Like sparklers on Twelfth Night thrown to the snowy dark
The Swede towns flicker bravely and go out
Five miles below on the sable parcels of night.
The Pratt & Whitney afterburners spout
Fire, then purr: descending through an arc
The aircraft touches down. End of flight.
Hardly a proselyte of heaven or anything
Like it, I stand in a ring
Of passengers waiting for baggage, crowding like swine
In a pen: I'm shaken to see, when bags of mine
Crash down the chute, how time the foreman picks
And chooses from the line
Of travelers in Minnesota at the Styx.

Who the man is, and how lonely lying here
Hobbled and cribbed in the elevator bed,
I can't imagine. Nobody. Anyone,
Whose silver hair unfolds from the slackening head
On pillow; no senator or financier
But boy fallen among Cadillacs; no fun
To find himself the one responsible, the boss,
At last not at a loss
For words. "Tea kettle . . . burglar . . . Spanish War . . ."

He slushes now in a voice half sigh half snore;
Cries then, "kill the rest"; defiance flashes
In his eyes as never before;
And kicks a nurse before his anger crashes.

With my brother and sister I stood
On the dock admiring the string of fish he held
Up for the camera
And us. He spoke that way
Or danced the messages
In tap shoes on the kitchen floor
Or said the Philadelphia Grapevine on his skates;
Preached elegance behind the wheel
As when he steered between the car he passed
And the moving-van oncoming.
He'd take his skates, the tap shoes
And the Shakespeare he had thumbed for years
And as he climbed the stairs
Flick off the lights, whatever
It was we were doing down there canceled.
Together we across the lake
Watched while he came heading in
Over the waters of Minnetonka,
Like Teddy Roosevelt on horseback
Careening down San Juan Hill;
Our father moving tall across the waves.
He stood in the rowboat, performing the forbidden;
His Johnson Seahorse outboard blustering on,
Whining when the hull slammed down
On the wakes of other fishermen who traipsed
Across this bay and that
Like little lords amain the sea
Making their names by conquering
The sunfish and the bass
As if freshwater fish were Spanish galleons;
Fathers in panamas on Sunday cruises,
Whole afternoons spent out of earshot, far

From the families on level lawns above the sand.
Through the lapis welter of the day
He came ashore,
The outboard idling to the dock;
Fixing us with an admiring eye,
His smile bursting us ajar, as he
Without a word held up his catch.

We did not turn (this was the dream) to drive
Around the block and back to our front door
But veered into a park, bucking the curb
Into the dark, where soldiers of the Great War
Stole past us, benighted silhouettes alive
With strobelike backflares, wary not to disturb
A wire or the superb composure of a mine,
The quiet kindled by the whine
Of an occasional artillery shell above.
You drove smoothly as ever, cognizant of
Each chuckhole; tightlipped, intent, cruising along
Without speech for love
Or me, into that stealthy, helmeted throng.

What time leaves behind is the high-tech of things.
Fat tubes like tentacles coil up from bruising
Needles in forearms to floats bobbing above
Two red-eyes volumetric pumps infusing
Lidocaine hydrochloride (which sweetly brings
Peace to the heart agitating for love)
And other potions of heal-all technologies
Which counter the disease
Of age, raise flesh from its stupor on the floor,
Proffer the derelict a coat, and pour
The life-supports—sucrose, potassium,
Heparin sodium chlor-
ide—into him, hot coffee for the homeless bum.

From the skewed mouth with a kind of howl
He mumbles, "damn you you are being cruel."
I wonder if he smells the mustard stench
Lapping everywhere. We're back at school,
Learning to hold still with Atenolol.
He claws at his monitor and tries to clench
It in his fingers, wrench it loose. The box that warns
If heart should fail adorns
His chest like an Olympic medal. In a blur
I see his sex lying there, too faint to stir,
Gray in a condom, cuffed with a little strap
Attached to a catheter;
Like a dead mouse in gray grass, head in a trap.

In teal shadows where breezes scarcely shook
The oak leaves, against the furrowed gray
Bark seamed with a moss inlay,
I saw him leaning with his book
Far from the machines
Of endless learning;
Delivered from routines.
He was returning
When he put down *The Merchant* and surveyed
The sultry field with daisies simmering
In the blue, replenishing
Midday. The day grew quiet by a hundred stages,
Scored with the braid
Of a blackbird's call
From cattails by the brook.
The singing there was small,
And the abandoned book
On its back lay open wide,
The breeze leafing slowly through the pages.

How I came slowly to his going then!
I heard the nurse long-distance telling me

The mottling and the cyanosis had begun.
I would not comprehend the urgency,
He was so strong, headstrong; strongest of men,
He'd stay among his three at least till one
At bedside, daughter or son,
Hugged him to speech, to bless
From his high wilderness
His child, but toiled then, now with joke, now rage.
At last it was mine to be next: to disengage
And sing, as the tenor, called to his loveliest
Work, brightens the stage
Alone and sings, by the dark hall possessed.

After a City Shower

The traffic brays, but the stalled horses
Calmly stare, exhaust in their nostrils,
As if they were hearing the wind's bel canto
In tall grass. Out of the horns of plenty
Banter drifts near *A La Vieille*

Russie: "move out," she tells him, "so don't
Go back." Her voice turns liquid, "allow me
To send you some." The silver parcels
And the practiced tintinnabula of hungers
Surround me; as much as wisdom I desire

The white rush of this intersection;
To take the meaning, once, of the corner
Of fashion. Tune to the man in gray flannel.
"Few people knew the true gentility
Of the czar and the czarevitch. But that

Was when." In the square the Beaux Arts fountain
Tumbles its effervescent helix
Of waters heaping, fogging the air
With scoops of mist that rise and vanish
In the brandy shadow of the Plaza's frieze.

On the blacktop where rainbows from oildrip mix
In puddles the rain left, people wait
For the light, then make their crossings. The Black,
Labored, kindled, leans into his own
Saxophone gold by the fountain's pool,

And I hum with him, hum his keening,
Lost so and found among the obsidian
Limos; one high, gridlocking strain
While twilight fords Manhattan, whose
Splayed wires thread each longing gaze.

Dinner for Two

The subtle and the obvious entwined
As they negotiated while they dined
Together. Other patrons, polyglot
Among the tables, faded, babbling prose,
Leaving them diachronic; at home with lines
Recalled across a silence.
      They had these lines
So old they seemed a home away from home.
Both melodies converged till one song rose
Like Venus, single from vociferous foam.

He feels he is running in place, pounding one spot,
His meaning being given, slowly, to love.
He is sweating. Distances always were pantomimes
Of credibility; when he moved toward them
They receded: or, as now, they fade and seem
To be what, earlier, was not. Sometimes
The mountain, on near inspection, becomes a glove;
The credible mountebank, a visored cloud;
The cloud, cloud-capped, becomes another cloud.
And she, first one foot then the other, slowed
In her place. Maybe she never ran for it, or jigged
Her jig. Familiar distances would fade
Into the latest view. The difference it made!
She began to think her whole part had been rigged.

Poor lovers, bargaining from privileged heads!
Their narrative typology was dead,
Roughly. For company, each brought a dream;
And all their variations drowned the theme.

Cabbage Days

Look how in heat waves the folding metal
Chairs go slack in the sun
And their withered arms settle
Waiting like ritual tongs to hold your body.

How their legs puncture the lawn
And the grass lies back, creeps on.
Think how the comfrey and mint
Will grow and cleave

Till it's time to bolt.
Look how the cabbages swelled
And now it is time to loosen carefully,
To give the feeder roots a severing jolt

With a twist of each head on its stalk
Detaining green
Increase in holding patterns
Until it is time to take them in.

Think how you, supple
On long afternoons, have lain in the sun
Or stood up
Glad not to be of use, not to be held.

Allegheny Front

Out of the dark, from a field over the valley, a cow calls.
In the quiet, the hoarse lowing crumbles from her throat
And fades. Silence again; each barn and star holds still.
Perhaps that voice the Allegheny hills echoed
Told of some pasture matter, or did it, late on the Sabbath
As the midnight drew near, declare a purge from the simple
Darkness of the traditions of men, the passing away
Of laws that had come to pass? I sensed the 1880

Town devout, how near each felt: the obedience
In holding hands; each channel free of interference
From tape, free of the tube unborn, not yet branding
Cerebral hemispheres with circuits indelible
As rust. In the glass negatives from the house on Main
That my friend printed, half the town—and two cows—pose,
The set jaws sweet. Those bumptious Chaucerian Baptists loved
Their fun but hadn't much, each gent his own Chanticleer.

But justification burgeons like sheaves bound in the rich
September of their fields, enough to make homes rosy
Through bellowing winters from Canada. The girls have scrubbed
And changed, entered; sat, stifling giggles, hands palm down
On taffeta skirts as if wiping, or spreading patterns;
The shopowner's coat, an upholstered tent, hangs off his body.
Mothers in pleats and ruchings of jet and blue cohere
In the chevrons of their blood. With no rouge or powder, faces

Shimmer as if the humidest day of summer chose them
To sit still or stand without moving, this task of recording
Saved for a day one stood there and watched the corn grow.
Perhaps their faces are glowing with other fire, celestial
Preenings, a sweat of salvation. The Spirit quickens, it whispers
In the pew, the surrey; it beats in the milkhouse pungent with curds
And sawdust in darkness; nasturtiums peek in at the door.
A visage looks on when they try on shoes and bend to peer

In patent leathers mirrored in polished blindnailed wood.
I was watching Emmanuel's land, where springs embroidered with vetch
Assemble, brim to trickle and stream to the still river
Where water, in shade of oak or storefront, flows or pools
By Main Street; falls two feet, crosses under a bridge
And courses on down-valley; mutters in white by mossy
Boulders, lapping the winding hillsides ruddy with clover,
Zoned with sheep. The thick-rumped fathers of Kankadea

Allowed the righteous to settle, swank as well as lame.
They would lay much aside at home; they became their ledgers,
Recorded each occasion, every possession; they
Had eggs on the spit, they were hunky dory; muscular
Never to hear what other men had done or were doing
In other places of the earth. The valley they chose
Smiled from limestone, cleaved to fossils of bivalve and snail;
And the paper of trellised flowers behind the nonagenarian

Is proved to be scored and peeling by the light raking
From the window with curtains parted at the left of the picture.
The family at the farm has spread a tablecloth of damask
On the lawn before they pose on it. Churches are plain
With little spires of tin, but the churches are many
And none abandoned. "Children," the minister cries, "can tell
Cheese from chalk; they know by God's grace how every kite
Has two requirements for flight: the wind that holds it high

And string to be rudder and guide its way; to be anchor
And hold it down. What is that string? Who holds that string?
Who can tell us today?" The pint-sized pinafored girl
Has been catechized, she flounces up the aisle beaming.
"The string is the Ten Commandments. Our Lord holds the string."
Her eyes rake the faithful, quaffing their approval.
The church, a barn with Greek trim nailed to the front, hulks,
A canal barge beached at an intersection of county roads

To which through waves of heat some forty or fifty souls
Carefully file, flushed and beleaguered in Sunday attire.
I climb the steps and enter a lobby with shelves of tracts
And a guest book, its thick wings spread. A cadre of ladies gives
An alarm of smiles; fluttering glances grapple among them
To find a stranger. In the heat of the Sabbath each lady
Conveys the militant, rosy assurance of an immortal.
Syrup of electric organ pours forth the *Old Hundredth*,

The minister-for-the-day stumbles among the verses
Of a psalm. One monitoring elder smacks his thigh,
He has taken color photos from his wallet for the Sabbath,
They are shut in the glove box of his Dodge locked in the sun.
The elders fidget, smooth their sky-blue suits and whisper
During a hymn, check out the scattered congregation
As if they are taking note of particular absences,
The stain of green and ocher lights on the pew that curves

Around no one; they pass the brass collection plates
That ring if given anything but folding money.
Over the bare, spackled walls the color of decrepit
Silk some flies randomly pause to lick, the sermon
Echoes as if down a tunnel; in a foreign tongue.
I cannot make out the sense. "One witness shall rise up . . ."
Finding freshwater words for the mouths of brute nature
As flanges hum in the great calefaction of all things

When the wise sunflower of dawn opens over the black
Collar of Allegheny horizon distantly pinned
With silos and crossroads; cumuli gaining shape with light,
Rose brothers of mountainsides. The highway sings,
A prism, the waxed gut of morning up from dreams
Out of the cushioned pews of cloud in rivering olive
Light. Carnelian hills! It is the Lord's Supper
The rough hand draws the dirty cloth from, brassy host

In salvers for his shaking hand. On the Southern tier
Out of the oak and maple woodland, out of the horn
Of modesty, skull and antler, sliced bellies of deer
Flame on the blacktop shoulders in the eyes of crows
On duty, picketing, holding their beaks wide, crowing, flapping
Their great black capes when I drive past. Believe the word
You do not hear. For the pause, the stutter of Sabbath,
Is awkward only, the silences are lively. The gift

Is blind. I kneel down, I begin to pray, I hear
My own authority, cool voice which says that beauty
Bears the numen, spirit rider. I am numb,
I am deaf. Mine are not laws, but feelings that earn
No bread in the milky valley, the pastel poverties
With their electric crosses and rayon memories
Saying grace from vestal mouths. At home, I wash and watch
The water braid to the marble basin, circle and pool.

Steel drums of heat sound overhead, thunders gather
Toward the cells of the monkish towns in mist-shrouded bottoms.
Town fathers plumb their doubts about wild instruments
But allow some laconic brass with fireworks on the Fourth.
It's still illegal on Saturday to stroll on Main,
Yet on Monday I'll find the living-color cards of men
And women coupling, laid back on subway turnstiles, behind
The sumptuous note cards with views of grazing thoroughbreds.

Keen as the semi's scrawl in the ears, swallows score
My sight, looping at evening toward chimneys of Kankadea,
To roofs swaybacked with terra cotta, imbricate tiles
Quoting an ancient world, a Mediterranean South;
Someone is playing a guitar, the melody floats from a Greek
Revival farmhouse. The night is a country church without
An ornament. A cow is lowing in the distance,
And telling the hour a bell in the white steeple answers.

Hesitation at Veterans Home

When May had come for keeps the veterans
Who walk out each morning
From the long wings
Took down the guard chain braced in the drive
All the low winter, and I took
My boy to visit
The deer park at Veterans Home.

                                        A wizened man there
Wearing a baseball hat
Liked the idea
Of watching a child come up close to the young
Buck whose velveted rack
Looked tender enough,
About to swell, almost tumescent. The deer
Flinched but licked the hand
Of my four-year-old,
Who let him have his way, enthralled by wildness.
The teeth are so small, just like
A person's, he said.
The deer licked him—wet to the elbow. What's
His name? the boy asked then.
Don't have a name,
The old man drawled.

                                My boy cannot stop looking
As he comes closer to this
Beyond. He cries then:
Eyeball to eyeball with the steadfast animal
That deer is nothing but
A pussycat,
The man in the hat declares, a pussycat.

The season is in earnest,
The gate in the fence
Is open now, where the deer graze, going through
Their old motions of foraging,
Ceaseless browsing
Though vets provide their fodder now. The deer

Have nothing to do, nothing
To fear, but now
And then a bawling baby, or an apprehensive
Street-smart kid from Brooklyn,
Or a small boy
Who cries to see what he is watching. The deer
Is patient, or tame, and gives
Great sloppy kisses.

Thatch

The man with arms who would hold them out
Might not know what a tree he seemed to be
To come for shelter to. Or then one day
He might, as chance decrees; and stop to wonder

Before an oak, inveterate huddler twisting
From storm or reaching sunward on its hill
When it found itself a kind of green veranda
For stragglers, bushed marines combing their hair,

A respite from the hot valley. This
Reticence he'd feel was like the quiet
Of a field when battle has moved onward
Elsewhere, and a strange calm on the long grass

Moves in as if earth shied, wounded, wincing;
And knelt, rooted, for nightfall and the stars.
He thought the reticence like the isolation
Of white dwarves, although a lesser, hardly

Cosmic rigor. He held himself erect.
The grass moved, the crickets in the grass
Stirred then as the grass he trod arched slowly back
Erect as it had been. Night rose; the grass,

The stonecrop, dragon's breath, the yellow asters
Rose up together from advancing shadows
Where the man walked on, imagining the refuge
He would come to, holding his arms wide now

As if to hug the stars, himself the refuge
He plodded toward, finding his body charged
With shade. The dark coursed through him, streamed beyond
Like direct current. Then he thought of those

Who came to him for shelter and how death
Was his accomplice now, the senior partner;
As once all dwellings had fire only, until
At length fire and darkness got discarded,

When men stopped watching them—began to live
In the high wattage of what they were doing.
Once everyone knew thatch, like dark, like fire,
Presences underfoot or overhead;

Everyone knew them, the rarity of them later
Was only our looking the other way. Only
The reticent man, holding his arms raised wide
Will find it as it was before it went quaint

And fossil, to be killed, like dust. Now he knows it:
Strong as wire, tender almost, a life
Surprised, because it was there all the time
Shy, smiling, asking with its dead lights.

Man in the Open Air

From the hollow, the wind soughing, down there
The mower's engine droned, veneering the slope
With a cloudburst of hay dust
Like a toy twister gaining on the orchard
Where he walked. At length

He stood where the accomplished animals had been
On the cut velvet their green hooves made
Padding long grass to grassy mold,
The neglected garden overthrown
By thistle, daisy, goldenrod. He heard

A cricket tick and watched it press its arms
Against September.
The season turned
In the rainless desert of itself,
Heroic summer canceled like a passion.

Now for the blank of cold, he thought;
Now throw the latch bolt, go and listen
For the chariot in the trees,
The groan of wheels
By the river when the stripped willows whimper

In the wind stroking above. There
In the eyes of limb stubs on the tree trunks
The wheels spin. In the far field
The mower rumbles its cage of blades
Naming the stubble, the cloud of dust.

*

A ghost settles there, like the ram's
Skull in the grass. Wild carrot
Unfurls through sockets,

Apotropaic stare unblinking, white
And white the chambered horn,
Spiral at last deciduous,

Flowing with bindweed; blown
To the powdery core. Look
Where the skull peers, the altered horn.

*

After the thunderstorm that night
Everywhere lay the forked, gray falls;
Soggy shuckings, lovely in fracture, strewn
Looking up from the sod as if stunned
Like runners clipped in mid career.

To Bingham Hill's unposted corners
The stripping westerlies reveal
Ebony wristbones of the apple,
The schist ribcage of an elm,
Creases of unmaking in a face.

Spider

The redwings have been calling this half hour;
    the sun, falling, will draw away
Their cries. Between the radiator and the sill
    an unhurried spider seems to look,

Wondering where to move. The bodiless head
    —or headless body—holds on to
The legs, a dome of small girders, arching.
    Then gripping the silk line he moves

Out, hand over hand down the grid, over
    and over the spaces set off by lines
Spun from the mouth. He rests before the sting,
    limbs lifting and falling, wrapping, keen

For the firefly mistaken there. The sun,
    beyond, was melting the last braid
Of branches in its eye. It canceled
    each scratch on the window I looked through.

I closed my eyes; there, islands of gold trailed
    across the blackness of closed lids.
The spider tied up his prey; hung there, gainly,
    at rest. The trees are a gray wall

Zoning the world. Downhill, a car speeds through
    the film of the visible. A small
Sublime of violence keeps streaming from him.
    The birds move off, and their song dies.

American Light

Through the expensive century
   Minute miraculars of Kensett
      Sifting green Newport waters
Charged the Third Beach with repose.
   Mooning Blakelock found diadems
      Where Indians encamped in acid groves
Elbowed original stars, the stars

   Fuse, numinous, round each form.
      The faultless clarity of light
A Hill or Church might postulate,
   Luminous untrammeled wild;
      Lane's tremulous Gloucester cove unmoving
Still as Plum Island's flat salt marsh
   Heade regarded and would

      Have folks remember given so
To lumberers, to Bierstadt's filmed
   Scintillant West easy as
      Driven savages to take,
Dissect: yet hardly picturesque
   Where spirit isolate wandered
      Contained, consoled by those

Perspectives improbably receding,
   The only vanishing point beyond
      Beyond. These were correlative
For pioneer profaning limits
   The mental shepherd of his
      Dumb hungers, overhanging
Desires extending "always" out.

Farsighted eye, luminous
Avenue for one bestial
So helpless urge to bless
And mutilating to consume
And evacuating never
To stand, breathe, occupy
Memorized one space for all

That too huge hemisphere!
Who settled to take home
A picture of some picture of it
Too sensible to that six feet
Amid such waste grace as all
These fallow these dark starlit
Valleys would leave to him.

Words for Dr. Richards

I.A.R.

"Seduction is a storm
Of calculating thought
Must surely be *proper form*
For bounders. Or it ought.
(How should I know, here,
With the heat of rhyme so near?)

"Sentiment's cold, I say.
Thought makes us energy
(If you turn it that way)
And heat. Some won't agree—
The young man can't, who fears
The thing unknown, the tears.

"New lovers chant and prate;
Package what's old, what's new
Outside them; recreate
What's in it (me) for you,
In you for me: relations
That instrument relations.

"Say he's not hard on her,
Just hard. Make no mistake.
His tiffs, his lusts were pure;
No violence is fake.
An instrument thought played
She was; a point he made.

"Then level with your lover.
Feel what knowledge you
Find mustering as you hover
Seeing what you're party to
(And the passion growing cold
As intelligence takes hold)."

*

Old men make testaments
Who know more than they tell.
But few, once done, commence
Their quest again, to dwell
On sense—and referee
Our suspect imagery.

Cold thought could not be true;
Mind's circuitry *not* lame,
Since hot: thought charging through
And through. Don't couple flame
To passion, nor reason freeze.
No identity in these!

The thought that rages right
Renews itself; re-forms
And formulates fresh light.
This man, this heart words warm!
Like the bush burning, thought
That burns does not burn thought.

Christo's Fence

Falling, to the insistence of gravity,
The sun from horizon touches the ivory
Felt of tall-crowned hats,
Sundown through Christo's dreaming
Fence that wimples
Oxblood over
The fawn dunes below of merino
Sheepfolds and Marin rock
Of goat-gray seabound light crashing
Softly against the windburned
Face of the rancher
Continuous with this place: he

Looks forth on pool, field, flock, mute
Luminous seam. Handy,
Ready, I want to look at, to ask him
What leaves he turns
In the vellum binding of choices made.
"I want to do this thing," wind buffeting
With calm firmness over
Him surviving the time he created,
Time he lives across, "I
Want to make the best thing." What
Else to know; men
In the corridors of their haste
Smiling with a wrinkle
At corners of a mouth that seems
For a moment to crumble a little,
Bits of crimson over the chin and bola
Tie like wine spilled; wanting to go
Back, back to the shagreen
Pasture where the posts stood
More in the pull
Of the wire than tall on a punky foot?

Continuous with the time
He hovers, the sheep lapels
Of coat smoulder
In the twilight wind, difficult man
Watching light dapple
The swooping skirts. The past
Passes like a helicopter of the state,
Free of feeling, checking
Him out, between the wind
And trammeled grass beneath our boots.

FROM
Thanksgiving Over the Water (1992)

Earth Day Story

I remember the dusty floorboards of wood in the streetcar
Of the Minneapolis Street Railway Company
And the varnished yellow banquettes of tight-knit rattan
Worn smooth by decades of passengers
The worn gleaming brass grips at the corners of the seats
And the motorman's little bell
Windows trembling in their casings as we crossed the avenue
Liberty dimes falling softly into the steel-rimmed hour glass
The gnarled hand of the motorman near.
My grandmother arranged herself against the seat
Her back as straight as a soldier's beside me
Her navy hat with velvet band
And net veil down making her head seem distant,
Her dreaming smile and the patient Roman nose,
A repose so deep; from my place
I watched her when we rode like princes
Rattling past traffic stopped on the granite cobbles
Riding downtown together, my hand in hers;
All that so much
That I love yet but feel no sadness for, that
Time crossed out like the trolley tracks taken up
Or entombed under the pliant blacktop of the modernized.

Beachcomber

He considered choice, which rocks among so many
He'd pick, on the shore of boulders and bare stones,
If he chose to take some, two or three more lovely
Than the lot, or simply standouts that caught his eye
For having unusual shapes.
                                        Off there they stood,
The couple he'd seen that morning, spiffy in matching
Madras jams and snow-white tank tops, drinking
Mineral water near the Mexican pottery,
The place mats and Noguchi lampshades, going at it;
The seeds of fear and hollow discontent
Shining and dark as black olives pouring
Across a table top, Manhattan pair
At the water's edge now, facing the horizon,
Swash and fleece of each spent wave wreathing
Their bare feet. They stood there now, crying out
To hear each other above the tumble of the surf.

When he walked by them, they fell silent; pretended
They were a pair of concrete mannequins
Propped there watching the view. Supposing he couldn't
Hear them on the wind at twenty paces, they
Started up again, moving on each other.
Flailed, accused each other; berserk, crying,
Red as if burned by feeling, raw under
Atlantic sun; wind; the overflights
Of curious dumpy herring gulls out shopping.
Soon he felt something tracking him, perhaps
A motor launch, perhaps a biplane trailing
Some message on a banner; an apprehension
From the blue, as if he had been chosen. One moment
A quaint answer came, of horsemen cantering
In the spray, a posse of ghostly heroes. And yet
He moseyed onward, checking the tideline, the stones;
And heading back in half an hour, blundered
Once more into that couple's shady business.
They shouted into the waves where the tide lapped.

He called to them (into the onshore wind,
Which shouldered his words a dozen ways), "You now,
Lay off the living well. Give a wide berth
To the dark wood of anger! Light, take care of them."
Before, he'd thought some posse might have tracked him;
He saw now what he'd heard, the cursive din
Of fly-overs by the Air National Guard
Was what it was. He turned his back. Over
His shoulder the engines droned, *you're out alone,*
To him, a man out walking, just nosing along.

The Tack

> Strait in are other chambers within
> chambers, the bottom of which no
> one has yet reached.
>
> —Coleridge

Pruning pine branches, lopping bittersweet June
Out back, bitten by some creature invisible
    Or just missed, this
Was down time. I rested under the inveterate
White pine, the dark shape on my arm draped blood,
Surprising crimson scarf, how soon a welt
As broad as a Mac, rising like inky dough!
    A small invasion,

Yet fear gunned through my limbs, a pinprick panic
The blood cried *run* to; then, *what have I caught,*
    What has caught me?
The odd sensation scouted through me casually
As a cancer; like a teenager high and wilding
On a spree. Inside the house then, inside a solace
Of walls, out of the unveiled threat of heat,
    Sun like a weight.

I sat there reading at the little desk
Facing the north wall; close there, dead ahead
    On the paneled wall,
The fresh gleam of a thumbtack, boss on pine,
Shone back its steely convex eye at me.
In the tack head I saw the bow window, bow seat, the plaid
Squab in the sun, all curving in sunlight, conforming
    To its circumference:

To my left, the darker hemisphere of chamber,
Like the bullseye of Arnolfini's wedding portrait,
    In shadow but gleaming
With hints of dresser and door ajar around me,
This face like anybody's in a convex mirror,

But tiny, far, a pinpoint in the shadows
Pulling me in. A self, shuffled under
    By a sudden other.

I watched the bruise mushroom. Coleridge, despairing
Because he'd fallen from his friend and turned
    From Sara; ill
And opium-numb—en route to the Siberia
Of tacky Malta—found terror, then found what
He'd hoped to find: in St. Michael's cave, the same
Chambers, the columns, the same chasm he'd
    Imagined, writing

Osorio. It was thus to his liking, those lofty wells;
So the stung pruner grew chummy with his swelling,
    What's happened here?
Unfolding to *hello, there!*, finding whatever
It was, was him now. Acceptance. The familiar;
This melting welcome, shy; reflexive; of
Such unaccounted-for increase to his
    Anatomy.

Then tender as a new baked loaf my old arm
Felt hardly part of me, bicep and bone
    Diminished under
The swelling's pillow. The beveled head of tack
No longer beamed a guttering eye; it was
Only a tack, flush with the wood, its wire
Needling deep, parting the tense pine fiber.
    When the fly stung

It was as if a curtain might have fallen,
Snuffing life out like a milkweed the wind sends
    Scudding to dust
And generations among the weeds; or I
As quickly disappear as a pricked balloon
One moment full of it, the next a tiny scumbag

Broken, moist on the needles under a pine
    Beside the road.

I watched how in the beady thumbtack's head
I was a millimeter shy of vanishing.
    The swelling held.
No pain. All right then. The floppy discs of memory
Kept printing feedback out, once meaningful
Segues now were synapses uncoupled:
A boyhood spanking; the homeless man in the subway
    Who talked with me;

The stray connections some deerfly had dredged up
Were nothing, though I kept falling through the net
    Of now, vertiginous.
My butt, he'd cried at ten on the rumpled bed
Though no one heard, for father had put up
The razor strop; hurried outside. The hurt
Was his possession. Those stings of guilt fell through him
    Like a slow rain.

That November when I went down below
To a soiled stillness, the cold platform stood
    Unechoing, empty,
Surrendered to a slow clock. I sat on a bench
Bent on my thoughts, the unabashed abandon
Of the city, in the streets the poor on watch
As from the hillside of abandonment;
    Deserted village

Of the collective heart, center ungrieving
And forsaken. When I looked up a panhandler—
    His ragged shape
Looming against the gray fluorescent twilight
Of that limbo station—stood before me; stood
In his pants—or his pants hung around him like

A voting booth. And he was in there somewhere,
    Making choices.

The beggar began then, bowing slightly, palms
Pressed together. I gave him—money. He said,
    "Bless you, young man."
He touched his hands to his lips—for the buck I gave—
And blessed me. My nod elicited first one
Then another remark about my goodness. I shrugged.
Out of the dark the boisterous train came on
    Pushing before it

The black air of the tunnel against us. The rest
Of his life and the rest of mine were about to be
    Two different things.
Under his filthy anorak he wore
A filthy undershirt, each stitch picked out
In grime; and the flesh was stained, and dark. Again
He bowed, "God bless you," and the track below gleamed
    With oncoming light.

And Coleridge, deep in the cave, saw "crown upon crown,
A tower of crowns, the models of trees in stone."
    Nature had doubled
An infinite beauty in his fantasies.
But they were imageless; rested in darkness until
His torch gave form to them. Here was a forest,
"A bushy-branched oak, all forms of ornament
    With niches for images

Not there." Whatever he found, first found itself
In him; there were no images now. Stalactite
    To stalagmite, drip
By cold calcareous drip. No vaulted chambers,
"No saints or angels." One shaft descended hundreds
Of feet, until "the smoke of torches became

Intolerable." And he rose for air to the blue,
    The resolute day.

Down there in his corner with dignity, the tramp
Bore witness, accosted me from the homeless land
    Emerging from nowhere,
From polluted night, like one of Van Gogh's miners,
Like the coal miner up from a Pennsylvania hill
Shining the little lamp on his forehead straight
In my startled face. "Here now," I said and took
    A ten from my wallet.

And handed it over. His last word died in the roar
Of the train arriving; I left him to wander, to con
    Or bless more travelers;
Yet watching the burnished thumbtack, tunnel mirror,
I caught his rushy odor still, the white wine
Of his urine; understood that blessings were; that I
Had been chosen, even as I was punctured by
    The awaited fly.

A Bamboo Brushpot

It was for my table, to put my pencils in
While I considered a fresh way to begin,
This brushpot chance had brought my way, a coarse
Bamboo copy of a Chinese emperor's
Minutely carved in boxwood. My bamboo showed
A mountain wall with billowing cliff that flowed
In tumult round its sides, then fell away—
Revealing a tableau of men at play.
It told of one who ruled well long ago:
Old Xie An, now seated at a low
Table; around him attendants in court dress;
All concentrating on a game of chess.

The minister would play, but he can hear
The sound of messengers, whose charioteer
Draws up his team around the bend. The horses
Neigh; the news is of vast enemy forces
Invading the northern frontier. Xie An plays;
Deliberation rules while he surveys
His partner's options, and the partner makes
His move. The game continues. A new day wakes
The far side of the wall. News from the North:
For two days victory flew back and forth;
Now Xie An has conquered. He refrains
From looking up. At the board his hand remains
Poised for a move. Aloof alike from word
Of victory or defeat, he has not stirred.

This botched pot's crudely carved, volume and line;
Of humble pulp that won't admit the fine
Detail that pleased an emperor once, and yet
That cloud-capped game's too earnest to forget.
May he continue play beside my chair
And I, to news just made, turn a deaf ear;
Go to confusion's bleachers as to school,
Greet squalid terror with stolidity;
And the cloudy invader with such deliberate cool
As showed an old man's skeptic mastery.

Abandoned Houses South of Stafford

Although you said there wasn't time I stopped
In Yorkshire, an intruder on the cattle
Grazing; tramped those grassy aisles and halls
Of Yorevale Abbey, ramparts of disaster,
Worn lattices of absence; tawny stone
Climbing the air. And here the stripped houses,

Bare clapboards the drifting weathers scoured, dry
Barracks for nothing—even disaster absent—
Brought back those elder ruins. The half-effaced
Facades stood up in the chilly apse of April
As if hung there from little swags of cirrus
Through the blue media of cold and light.

Since you had gone, I went to look, desiring
The walk, if that was what there was, on weekends.
The rocked walls rode on the momentous soil;
In the sun some wisps of wallpaper would flutter
From an upper room's plaster-and-lath that leaned
Crazily under the stress of beam and stud,

Hung on like petals to a blossom blown.
Doorframes with fluted column, delicate cornices,
Panes of an Adam fanlight framed the meadows;
Windows opened on cows, the eyes of cows
Opening on windows; in a pasture, houses tumbling
Like the abbey among cows grazing Yorevale field.

Glisterings off the lake downhill flickered, lapped
At gravestones leaning like the abandoned dwellings
Back in Stafford—liver spotted marble
From Vermont, red slate, Connecticut sandstone; grass
Crowded some fallen markers laid out level
As hearthstones, lifting them so they rose like lids

Opening; while other flags descending sank
Under the radiant blank of windy sky;
Dipped below turf, thick hanks of green scrolling
Them over. I froze to see; for you had gone;
For the derelict earth was warm, and young; the doors
Framing those meadows, meadows framing those doors.

Place and Fame

1

When I was eighteen and he came
To "say his poems" Robert Frost
Stayed in the memorial guest suite
Tiny wing off a great brick dorm
Decked out with shutters and cedarshakes
To look like an eighteenth-century cape
With flowers and a knee-high picket fence
Around the dooryard, very private
And not to be approached by us.
Once each year he came, one year
He arrived three times, always by ten
In the morning, when he vanished
Into the cottage to prepare himself
For his appearance at the end of the day.
One time the master's wife revealed
That he took nothing in his retreat
But three raw eggs, always three
Raw eggs. Gently mystified
She said she thought he put them down
The toilet (shells and all) and then
He'd open up the clandestine roast
Beef sandwich stowed in his bag of poems.

2

When Noland put The Gully up
For sale he had no takers until
The National Register listed it—
The farm Frost owned for twenty years.
When a celebrity producer
Had finally bought it and made it more
Like home (in the manner of Bel Air)
It flowered in chintz; enough pillows
To bed a cast. He found this sign

At a local shop, *By All Description*
This Should Be The Place the legend read.
It was Victorian, the owner's pride
And joy, her trademark and the one
Item (Meg told me more than once)
She would never sell, no matter what.
She sold it for a hundred bucks when he
Had a replica made for her, and no one
Guessed her famous sign was a repro
Unless he happened to check the original
In the bricky foyer of The Gully.

3

Time counts, and time was counting when I once
Met Frost at Homer Noble Farm. He'd been
Through Kennedy's inauguration and was
About to go to Russia for the President.
Ann Gentry was cooking dinner for eight, and I
Was carefully coming down the steep stairs
When he appeared from his uphill studio.
Late sun reddened the famous face he wore
In front of the taut face I felt his eyes
Peered at me from. Under the open shirt
The wrestler's shoulders sloped with age to arms,
To hands, spread fingers holding in each grip
A huge uprooted head of lettuce, roots
Still shedding gobbets of earth on the step at his door.
"So you're the guest," he said, "and I don't know
Your name." I gave my name. He'd not remember,
For I'd been only a boy in a room of boys.
"I've got the salad from my garden here.
My contribution. Maybe you'll take it in to Ann."
Behind him in shade toddled John Berryman.

4

Frost ate, and when he wasn't eating, talked.
He let you know he knew about baseball.
He said he was thinking over what he'd tell
Khrushchev after he'd said him "Mending Wall."
After Ann's sirloin, the salad and the wine,
After ice cream on cantaloupe and cake
We sat around the living room drinking gin
Though Frost drank glasses of rum and lemonade
With a splash of sugar, which I was appointed to bring.
Now Berryman and Frost on opposite ends
Of the swaybacked Empire sofa eyed each other
And the long upholstered void between them. "What
Ever happened," said Berryman, "anyway,
To Empson? You knew him in England did you not?"
John fixing him with a cool stare then, Frost
Hung fire, some of us thinking how Empson was
At work in England that very minute, when
At length Frost drew the hand that held his glass
Along the sofa's back toward John and looked him
In the eye and said, "some of us pass by."

5

In the noontide of his powers,
A boy's will coupled with the man's
    Achievement, he drove round town
Delivering his son's cut flowers—
Just like a pair of also-rans
    To set up (father and son)

    As florists in Vermont!—
Was what folks whispered, though he was
    Just helping out he'd say
On every morning's floral jaunt

Through Bennington, Main Street abuzz
    To see the great bouquet

    His Packard had become.
He did not say he drove for love,
    No more could estimate
The little, local vacuum
For letters, or the town's gossip of
    His yen for real estate.

    One day a woman called
From the Catamount to him in his roadster,
    Deliveries at the side
Door!—told him, who had enthralled
London; told him, the very lodestar
    Of the countryside, astride

    Their narrow valley like
The genius of the place, at peace
    And home where he was born!
He was impressed that she could strike
Home so simply. It might release
    Him from this wild, forlorn

    Routine he'd taken on,
Thinking about his place in town
    And trying to help his son.
At The Gully farm on the high lawn
He pondered. The boy was so cast down.
    What he could do, he'd done.

Trifid

In the building of glass, in the city's
Dutiful violence of heights
The man once blond
Enjoys the day that is his
Aroused while he works
Writing checks
And watches blue sky out his windows
And far below, the swarming highways, the busy river
Quicksilver under the light of noon.

*

Chill evening, I listen to the motor;
Switch on the headlights in the early dark.
For a time I sit in the car before going
As I wonder about the fuel running out,
And the power; cruelty
Of megawatts to birds
And maples shriveling on the hill.
Sentiment in a jar, I think; and still
I ask if I'll get through without a hitch
Before I am out in the cold
In the dark with only the dogs.
Chill evening, I listen to the motor,
I can watch my breath
And see the dogs running, crossing my lights
Like white wolves in front of me
Through the darkened neighborhood
Barking, roaming.

*

Some doughboys are mugging for the camera
Grinning; someone
Is handing out letters randomly. Any letter
To any soldier. Fresh troops come up
To take letters. Clearly the letters
Are all from home and all counterfeit;
This filmed grouping is propaganda, serious

Footage to use Stateside. Now
The soldiers are laughing

Through tears,
Their limbs do not follow them
To the ambulance. They keep in line
Hands laid on shoulders, eye-blisters
Wrapped in bedsheet bandages.
In a shaded ward the amputees
Are smiling, smiling. Because
It tickles? They are going home? Because
They are idiots?
Smile away, Yank, beautiful boy,
Your fresh stump humming!

Tyros

1

On the Navy base
Everyone stood in his rank
Wearing white cotton
Bellbottom trousers and white
Blouses each with one
Chevron, or half one chevron.
This was in the wind,
On parade. The wind gently
Flapped the white, slapping
Limbs randomly, flashes of
White cotton. No one
Said anything for hours
It seemed, except, "I
Have to piss" in stage whispers;
Stood at attention
First, then at parade rest, in
Bright sun, blue breeze.
The formation was broken
Fifteen minutes before noon.

2

You may remember
    when you were in boot camp pent
An Army recruit
    on deep-sink the livelong day
Of KP, old rags
    long wet in the number ten
Cans under that sink
    were white and soft as boiled rice
With maggots slowly
    afoot; from which vision of
Your little problem
    you were torn by the far-off

Bark of the head cook
      sending you to some fresh air
      under the full moon, and sleep.

3

In boot camp they were once
marched to sick bay; seated
in a scoured lobby to wait
for vaccine and a wanton
Yellow fever shot
should they be sent to Asia.

It was one more hurry-up-
and-wait line, ennui of mud
on boots, drying to powder.
And strapped to a gurney there
in the hall, on center stage,
untrousered, a man lay, prone.

The buried agenda of pain,
of power grew manifest.
The doctor was to do
his spinal tap soon now
and there, obedient, they sat
receiving this bit of training

by means of visual—and soon
audible—aids as the doctor
held up the needle, long
as a dipstick, checking it
by the strip of fluorescent light
in the hall painted neutral gray.

Dispensing with anesthetic
he went to work and eased

the needle home. The gasps
of pain grew more, tormenting
the ammoniated air,
though in modesty the man

had turned his face to the wall
away from the boys' eyes,
bug-eyed recruits who followed
orders, waiting turns
to step up, as the captain said,
step up, step up like a man.

Gulf Memo

Tell me the way to the wedding
Tell me the way to the war,
Tell me the needle you're threading
I won't raise my voice anymore.

And tell me what axe you are grinding
Where the boy on bivouac believes,
What reel you are unwinding
For the girl in her bed who grieves.

While behind a derrick's girder
He watches the sinking sun,
He asks what he'll do for murder
And what he will do for fun.

Will you read him the ways of war
His Miranda rights in sin,
Will you tell him what to ignore
When he studies your discipline?

He dozes off—but he shakes
In a dream that he is the one
Death finds abed and wakes
Just as the night is done.

Tell me what boats go ashore
Riding the oil-dimmed tide,
Red streamers and black in store
For the boy with a pain in his side.

And tell me where they are heading
Tonight; now tell me the score.
Tell me the way to their wedding
I won't raise my voice anymore.

The Second Law

Beside the bed I watch
            His hindered face
The dented cheeks lifting
            And falling
Scarcely perceived, with the stroking,
            The curbed
Breathing. I hold the mug of black
            Coffee fresh
From the nurse's station heat
            Is working its
Arduous way through the glazed
            China wall

To my cold hand. Soon
            It is too hot
To hold, I put it down
            And I take
The colder hand in mine
            And I wonder

If it is taking any warmth
            From mine
Or if his chill alone
            Is oozing
Through the wall of our grip our
            Holding on. I
Stand outside the bars through which
            The gaze clings
And the stubble crowning the sheet
            And the jailed
Knowing, letting him, letting him
            Go.

Father and the Minneapolis Chacmool

This postcard shows you gaming, eyeing four players, each
Of them you in the poker game faked with mirrors, your
Solitaire changed to the macho game of five card stud,
Your hair in the photo slicked down so neat in 1930
Eyeing your opponents, each at first appearance
A different man, each dapper as a dictator, each you.
And where will I meet you, now you have gone to the dead below?

Can it be? The Minneapolis Chacmool, unveiled, is fake.
That eyes-right corker I'd adored since childhood, leering
At the Chinese tomb guardians staring through the sun
In the next gallery back at him: the label notes
He has been "widely exhibited here and abroad" yet now
They know: not some recarving merely of the face
Or prosthetic limb to double for one broken off

One high noon of bloodlust revelry in elder Mexico
But the entire sculpture, made for market, skull to toe:
An old con man craning his head over his shoulder
Like a peeping Tom—like you, Father—on a chock-full beach.
The Chacmool right as rain wears latticed sandals; holds
A bowl for the priest in his lap: the red hand of the priest
Would ease his grip on the turquoise haft of the jade dirk

With spalled green blade and hold aloft the steaming slick
Heart sliced from the winning youth; and place it there;
But this one is barefoot, and his hands lie empty now,
Limp on the dusty lap, a sort of driving cap square
On the crown of his giddy head, shading a general's gaze.
They seemed so genuine we shook when they went wrong.
Old man, I wish you well; old man, I send you love.

Walking from Grasmere

Running up the browsed hillsides
Over the hillocky pasture lots
Unfallen walls wove courses,
Repeating mud-hued stones
The ridged copings rhythmic there
Like the backbones of Brontosaurs

A herd where it fell
Freezing, benighted or famished, inert
Silent as the muddy sheep
That fed along the combed slope
Or sprawled, legless wool-sacks
Growing from sod. Overhead

Out of the steelwool cloud cover
Low into the spacious afternoon
Red as a redcoat a jet fighter
Gouged loud into the valley;
Out. It saturated all
With echoes from afar

Knouting the air,
A name of sound for all
That prim, enduring world.
I looked up, back, knowing
My thoughts like the stone sheep
Like that potted landscape were the past.

To a Mantis

It's as if I hear far-off cries; I turn
    To the shelf
Where the mantis eggs lay, forgotten, three
    Hundred eggs
From Pennsylvania in a taped box marked
    Beneficial
Insects, from which one has crawled now and stands
    On the lid
Wobbling and tiny in the kitchen warmth
    Like a scumble
Of spider web; yet arms outstretched as if
    To hold
A fly, Martian eyes peeled; this waif ready
    To help
In the yard: and three hundred more inside.
    Outdoors
With them now! Finding half of them dead, cooked
    In my kitchen,
I spread the rest on honeysuckle, spruce,
    A swale
Of sourgrass where an elm stump rotted.
    Cold night
Gone by, a little band not quite dead yet
    From exposure,
Small as the mosquitoes they'd save me from,
    Quivers
And stretches in the small bowers, swelling
    With dew,
Tottering on their posterior limbs
    Apparently
Watching some ants that carry off their dead
    Brethren
For supper. These more than underprivileged
    Lives feel
Some whiff of joy in the foolish breeze, and
    Turned now

I toward this world feel exaltation, here
        In this little
System, motherless blinkers in the wind
        Of demise.
In two days, even the living have flown
        To hiding
Or death, I do not know. O brother sun,
        Warm this
Honeysuckle; sister honeysuckle,
        Shelter,
Give honey to the mantis. O brother
        Mantis,
Grow, devour the pests; be at home, stay
        In my yard!

Thanksgiving Over the Water

The master cylinder of my cherished new
Secondhand Valiant is leaking.
My pedal goes to the floor already,

The slave cylinders do not respond, an ordinary
Experience obtained by ordinary
Commercial transaction. I am justified

If after paying for a replacement I feel
That this experience has not been real
Enough. And I may turn

To ordinary experience on a higher plane. The rain
Is gleaming on the slates
Of the barn where through a mist a wave

Of evening is falling, brightening
The thin, smooth stones. This brings me
Less complicated thoughts, notions

Perhaps archaic on this modern evening, modes
Of conceiving the effects of time
On space. Beauty is difficult, said Beardsley

Whose brief life and anguish in furnished parlors
Made him belong to a becoming
In which he found himself to be

Not himself. I think of the sculptor,
My friend, whose otherworldly metal
Intensities kept on when his strong hand

Began to turn, quelled in an ill wind;
Who never spoke the trying, holding
Pieces together; and watched the fields gone to scrub,

For everything changes to something else. The barn
That once held animals and hay
Yet houses lively creatures, and hay,

Though creatures a thousand times smaller, the hay
Too rotten to use except as mulch;
Just now, the haunt of bees: my barn

Stands brooding, stalled like an arthritic
Dinosaur in the rain. Over against this
Dry husk, dry under the hammered lapping

Of protecting slates and rafters, wings
Of carefully feathered stones, is a world
Which is not timeless so, if such a rhythmic

Pattern in the oiled, after-shower light may be
Considered timeless; or merely a figure
Of order that gleams beyond reckoning;

Beyond one's clocks and cruxes—beyond
Or in the foreground, other world
Where all is, always, of the moment.

Similarly the illusion of space with limits
Withers in loping fences, falling
Boundary markers lost whether ledge or cherry,

Rectangular fields eroded by curling waves
Of vegetation with "other plans," a surf
Of sumac, white pine, aspen; and I am grateful

For circuits of *there* becoming *here*, the precise
Area, say, of the blue surface of a car
Contained for a minute by a focus of consciousness,

The blue surface of a blue car then slowly
Going to brown, running to earth, the sky
Where it touches down as pools underfoot; as if smoke

In a rut of rainwater; dimples of rust, rising
Bursting the surface calm of the blue as blisters,
Golden atolls that never sleep: at the center

Of the illusion, the moving waters, the reward.

Fort Burial

The boy was eight and came running
From the box elder woods; he cried, "Hey, Dad,
You want to help me organize
    A mole funeral?"
The sun was going. I said I would,
Sure thing, as soon as I stopped raking.
He waited; then—he disappeared.
    I found him inside
In the kitchen, on his mother's lap
In tears. He stood then, thinking; some tears,
But thinking, mostly, about the dead;
    A proper burial
Of the mole. For coffin he chose a box
Blank checks had come in; a winding sheet
Of tissue; to garnish the lid a sprig
    Of bittersweet:
Long mole, plump prodigal, with pelt
Of midnight-glossy fur, like a ruff
Engraved by Hollar, clenched coral feet
    With Meissen claws
Minute, pink, and fragile-looking;
Yet ferocious in the power I felt
They barely now had given up,
    A moonless drudge
Whose silken frame meant business only,
My son considered it on its bier,
Stroked the fur sweet to him now
    As his stuffed toys.
I fetched the spade; we buried it
By the edge of the field in a clump of sumac,
A bower the boy had named *the fort*.
    He found a crate slat
To mark the grave: with a nail on the pine
He scribed a legend: "In this Hole
Lies my Mole." Mercy, he
    Inscribed the grave!

He scored the words in deep—and smiled.
In half a twilight hour he
Had tried the work of mourning on;
   A death for the heart.

On the Street

Sometimes, thinking of you eaten by absence,
When the square whitens with shoots of spiraea,
The sun mercuric on ouzo and water,
I stand on the steps with desire.

When the square whitens with shoots of spiraea
A whiff of exhaust smudges the air;
I stand on the steps with desire
Taking comfort in an earth which is powerless.

A whiff of exhaust smudges the air
Past the window in flower, the flowery walk.
Taking comfort in an earth which is powerless.
I want to do the right thing, I want to go back

Past the window in flower, the flowery walk.
Forgetting the broken key of your face
I want to do the right thing. I want to go back
And see the day through desire.

Forgetting the broken key of your face
I stand on the steps in the licorice sun
And see the day through desire
Watching the boys on the square play touch.

I stand on the steps in the licorice sun
Sometimes, thinking of you eaten by absence,
Watching the boys on the square play touch,
The sun mercuric on ouzo and water.

Around Our Table

Stephen Fels, 1940–1989

He was coming out of the dark
To join us at our picnic table,
He was about to head back down
The thin corridors of waiting.
He might have cried, "I don't need Belsen,
I have my body." Instead he called,
"You may not recognize me, I
Am Stephen. I came to see you anyway."
But right away I knew the bones,
A quiet incandescence in our midst,
His face in a glow like a straining runner's
In the little light our candles made.

You who came through the August dark,
Who came to us without your hair,
Without color, scarcely with flesh,
You walked around the corner to us
And cried, "hello there" in the dark;
Before we could see, you called our names.
"You are Geoffrey, you are James,
You're Kate." We did not know how joy
And fear could come together so
As one; in the unfeeling breeze
Of the unspeakable, your bright face
Like a lamp in the dark around our table.

And that was something, as one who finds
His father, years perhaps beyond
His death, in subway or crowded street,
A presence felt that may tell something
Or tell nothing, some commission
Or timely caution from beyond
The grave, or maybe none; one who

In his devotion plays the fool
And fails to comprehend, just yet,
What he must do. Stephen, you were
The message we waited for, glowing face
Like a lamp in the dark around our table.

Mother's Day

Back from the round of visits, I take
The straight-edge spade and the steel rake
And start by cutting in and slicing under
The turf, lifting the pared squares.
Heaving rectangles, triangles, odd
Clumps of green earth-skin away
To plant a tree here, add grass there;
Trundling loads in the wheelbarrow
Around back, fitting them in again,
Tucking them back (friable selvage
Of drying root-strung loam pellets,
Dribble from earthen soffits, hanging
Like bangles from Grendel's necklace). I push
And pat, snugging them close together
As if bedding bricks up in mortar
At the spread and slap of the trowel, kneading
The roughly sifted dirt in, pulling
Sinewy taproots of dandelion,
The insidious net of bittersweet fuse
Snaking in the hush of soil to blossom;
Then the tamping down with booted feet,
Lightly springing my body, lightly
Beating earth with an easy measure;
Connecting the hose with rusty couplings
Stiff from winter, washers brittle
Or gone altogether, slobbering; then
Hosing the ground, soaking the sods that look
As if pleased to be hugging earth again
—Heavy they lie, pressing warm dirt!—
Letting the water play over the sods,
Washing them green, sogging them in,
Now while the streams are mingling over
The mosaic of living pieces knit up
In a strange bed, clods no more aware
Of where they once were than where they are,
Indistinguishable in a week from grass
They're bedded next to, now I watch

The new flies gather for their first rally
Of the season, swarm on the rim of the blue
Wheelbarrow. There at the hedgerow, under
The maple sprouts making ready to leaf
But still gray sticks in the gray ground
I watch ajuga, hosta, fiddleheads coming,
Taking tentative looks at the new world;
And hear the redwings calling, and the robins;
Strange: after drear dark the strange, sweet
Business of the birds overhead once more.

American Days

NEW POEMS

Threads

Bolts

The logs of wool jersey plastered with labels
Lay in the lint and litter, columns in a heap
Like a Doric temple left at the shipping dock,
Trucked in from Dan River.
                        They smelled so sweet,
Concentric rings like cross sections of a tree;
But these would shrink, unwound on the cutting block
Long as an alley to the boy who wheeled them in.
Whistling finale, faille unrolled on the table's
Spotlit runway, layer on layer, flat
For the cutter's saw following paper template
To carve out panels of dresses, thirty deep.
    That trade, like subsistence farming through thick and thin;
The rounds of seasons, this year's style or that
Year's loss; core sample of eternity.

1945

Ribbed faille sings out when it unrolls across
Itself; bolt after bolt lay up, unite
For the blade of Izzy, like a doctor dressed in white,
Sleeves starchly rolled up burly arms; the hum
And glitter of the little circular knife
Softly screaming through reds and tawny umbers
And a sheaf of special orders, orchid and plum;
Glazed taffeta slides, but wool packs tight like moss
For the muscular fist gripping the steel. Rosa,
Testy assistant, baleful refugee,
Helps Izzy—and only Yiddish between them. She
Must keep one sleeve rolled over the indigo.
Tattoo: but after work would show its numbers,
Inky brand of her undeniable life.

Shipping Boy

Bald Applebaum of Shipping sampling lunch.
Your Virgil and your boss down those dark aisles,
From his wire cage—riffling through order files
With a licked finger—barked: forget it, the Punch
And Judy!—whatever looked too good to him
He called *the Punch & Judy*. Crocodile
Tears, that was her *shtick*; and then the smiles!
It was all *chutzpah*, Rosa playing it so grim.
He stirred his soup with awful satisfaction.
Stirring with pride or failure—hoping to score
From the dark of the back office—warned: she taunts
You; she's a designer; you are the attraction;
The boss's boy better get over it before
She bares you her arm and gets just what she wants.

Lunchbox

Tin lunchbox open, she smokes and watches out
The eighth floor window. Pigeon; sky; one cloud.
Watches her forearm and sees nothing but—
Nothing. Dull parchment of untanned skin.
What morning music is this place about
She wonders, as the distance they've allowed
Her grows in this limbo where the door is shut
On the living; for now is for the dead, for kin,
For smoke and looking down at odors, where sweet-
Smelling threads and swags of lint coax a cough.
The numbers do not float away like dust,
Lint dust that swirls with operators' sweat
Billowing from machines someone turns off;
These strange "girls," how innocent and robust.

Downstairs My Son

Downstairs my son this very night
Embarks on his eleventh year;
Watches a movie on cassette
With six boys, most eleven, all
Crashing from horseplay after cake
And pizza: crowded before the tube
They are in thrall to the brave crew
Whose Flying Fortress bombs the hell
Out of those German factories.
But soon the enemy makes good;
Some flak strikes home; a gunner now
Is hit in the chest, falls back as if
He's tackled in a game. But then
Cries out; screaming, he twists in pain.
The boys stop bouncing, cheering; they
Fall silent. Then the gunner, dead.
Dogfights between some Messerschmidts
And British Spits lighten the mood
Toward violence; the old team sport
Of fighting by machine. Tonight
The boy stayed up—how tenderly
Staving off sleep—to be alert
On the anniversary of that
Very minute he entered life:
But fell asleep, just all played out
From play, his stringy body dead
To the world before the hour came round.

Mogadishu Mon Amour

The wrathful boys must drag it trussed with rope
Jigging around their city, thirsty world;
Dusty shape, body road stones strip.
I budge, wedge breath down; must clamor must
Find it, a word flawed word for that flaunting
This losing face—body exhibited
Savaged. Sighing for the young dead I want
Vengeance on vengeful boys whose rage is hurled
On him, on me, taunting with gun and vaunting
Arm. Then woe, the weighted body, lust
(Folded under the last social motion,
Find it sleeping like a dog in the sun)—I want
To be with him, naked body dead;
In secret want the innocent submission.

Watching the Purge

The lieutenant is to be

shot as an example. Our
tree is full of birds, black notes.
The mail truck shudders past
dispersing outward a slow-motion
shrapnel, scoring the sky.

The air fills up with war
invisible. Turn the switch
the snow diminishes
waves clear then with its rusty cuspids
the tank quarters a girl.

The bird is full of trees.
Songs and berries, nests. Black trucks
inch past the arctic rocks
where birds lie, eyes trained on the deep sky.
My lieutenant asks to

be made an example of.

A Common

He is crisp, hard from a mold, a Romanesque
Peering from his low-arched niche
Like a Coptic clerk behind his desk
In a grave relief. Popeyed, suppressing an itch

To move but smiling, he is thinking about
Retreating once more inside his little friary.
Staring from the couch of fever along his bones,
Perhaps he will read *A Tale of My Hut*

Or the fiercely Bostonian Inman *Diary*.
He will walk instead; bravely—the lightly shaken hand—
By the iron fence, committed to getting there alone
Across the park, alert for the first last stand.

Down the walk from the children who misbehave,
The generosity of the trees. These answer
The shouting with shade; they offer bandana waves
Above her there, quick as a dancer, a dancer

Always a dancer, mother of sixth-grade bold
And balky boys. Heeled with renunciations
She talks with him, single and single; old,
Conversing above the feverfew and lupines.

Hard By

Taking the westward walk at sundown now
She looks across the field back of the house
And catches liquid reflections of the sun
That sets in her windows, tingling sockets aflame,
Fake little conflagrations mimicking how
Everything might go—interiors shake loose,
Belongings turn to shadows one by one.
There stood the chest she loves, and oak bedstead;
Corners familiar things brightened become
Ash-white; the sash and lights now faceted
With crimsons lapping. As good as gone, the rooms
They'd soundly slept in, and the locked front door.
But the sun will set, she knows; its ruddy dooms
Be snuffed like matches, low windows dark once more.

Forked Animal

The rounds of unwashed dishes cease
Their chatter from the sink.
He feels their strange unease
And he stops moving, too.

Imperceptibly the earth moves
But still it moves; for him
And for the rat that leaps
In the dark, on guard, on a whim.

Soon now the house will get the shakes.
It may be a house of cards
Yet some defiance wakes
In the cellar, gritty sounds

Like gravel tossed in a can. The earth
Is on a rumble, like a tied
Half-broken horse that kicks.
Not yet for men to ride

It groans, not up to much; half calm
Like the sea as it laps at its rim.
The house is a house of cards
And the rat will comfort him.

A Walk-In Orrery

John Swan

I'm here to see this model of the spheres
where our planets make a cosmos that just fits
inside the circular room; a folly
of the Enlightenment. But your bout with death
is what I'm thinking of, resistlessly as gravity
holding you like a moon in thrall to its

sovereign mass while we, a little out of breath,
like lightweight meteors flit and skitter,
trail sparkles of reflexive fear across
the dark. And you, not lonely and (you said) not bitter
and not (I thought) afraid, too soon will make
your move. But enough of melancholy!

I'm here with an old friend. We're out
to show me a good time, and music plays,
if not the music of the spheres; some moody violins
romance us. A button beckons, red, ablaze
with inner light. I touch it, and the dim-bulb sun
goes even dimmer. We sit back. The show begins.

Across the cosmic mock-up, metal quarrons ride
in cold pursuit, seeming to importune
each other. Everything rotates—save for Saturn, which
inches along so slowly we decide
they didn't throw his switch.
Green-landed, sea-blue Earth with her white moon

spins furiously, showing off. And Mars
is racing, furtive, like a baseball caught
in the drag of something else's gravity.
A recorded voice intones the facts with practiced awe.
And then the whole contraption crashes with a
clunk. Is heaven kayoed—seeing stars—

or what? The planets one by one
shake lightly on their spindles of black wire
like ornaments on a tree that shudders
when the dog brushes against it. Well, this was fun.
The music starts to fade. And you'll be gone
before I write the lines you asked me for.

But poems are only a raid
on the inevitable. The machinery of my life,
you said last month, is slowing
and when the stress becomes too great
for those who keep it going,
adjustments will have to be made.

Our lines do not have answers, framed
and cunning as may be. Not to phrase
too many questions may be best; and steer for home
clear of ignorant hankering. Let your wishes
like those baubles near the dome
go their entropic ways. And have good days.

Hogback Lookout

Mid-August at Hogback Lookout, ample
      nature is standing still. Outside
           where three pay telescopes and one

Phone booth wait for clients, the high
      promontories stand watch at noon.
           Inside the shop, our fauna of Vermont—

Red fox, gray squirrel, Canadian lynx—
      hold their poses and do not sniff
           the small museum's musty air

In which the taxidermist (who owns
      the shop next door) exhibits them. On guard
           at the porcelain of the urinal

A Daddy Long Legs, old as a stone,
      has waited here, motionless
           hour by hour, week upon week.

Outside, in the wind a girl is clutching
      her white blouse. She stands by the pay phone
           which perches in the weather

On the wooden trestles of a deck above
      valleys where the hawk hovers and swoops
           in the hot light, perpetual blue;

Now the phone where she is standing looking
      out on the steep air is ringing,
           ringing; and she stands there, not moving.

The Change

Those yews at winter's end,
Near black on snow—she said
As they walked—are proper green
For the shutters of a house.

He wondered, walking there
Watching the feint and dart
Of sparrows returned to stark
Hedgerows, alighting on canes

Of blackberry thorned and bare.
As they walked they thought how quiet
This end of winter was,
How long, both of them watching

The neutral tones of March:
The slow, ferocious patience
Of air and plant and bird
Slowly squaring with change

And change. Without a word
They watched the sky, blank now,
Muzzled in iron gray
As if some brighter world

Had sealed its doors on theirs.
He wondered how the season
With this imperious pause
Changed imperceptibly

And answered her—now half
A mile beyond those yews—
That their winter hue was right
For the shutters of a house

But that the yews would change:
An emerald rise from earth's
Dark core, needles leaden
With cold, soon brightening.

Mexican Head

The terracotta head from Teotihuacan
With his smiling grimace is still with me.
I picked it out of a cigar box full of this-and-that
On Third Avenue when I was seventeen.
I remember the Third Avenue El outside

Roaring above me at the window of the shop
When I sifted the jumble of minor antiquities
For something to take along, to hold.
Behind the little head on my shelf I find
A cluster of eight egg casings that a wasp

Has sealed to the clay, gray as the clay;
Popped open now, little ones hatched, buzzing free
Into the close air of my office
And out the opened window, up into the sky
To toss and carry in the wind they know.

The World

Running home
     in the dark
          barefoot

From a wedding
     party at the big house
          his daughter nine years old

Met up with someone's
     half rooted
          property stake

The winged flange
     swiped at her
          ankle

A crescent
     wound bleeding
          when she walked

In to them smiling she
     had not
          noticed it yet.

Photo of Melville; Back Room, Old Bookstore

I passed him by at first. From the photograph
Peered sepia eyes, blindered, unappeased
From a lair of brows and beard: one not amazed
At anything, as if to have looked enough
Then turned aside worked best for him—as if
Night vision was the discipline that eased
The weight of what he saw. A man's gaze posed
Too long in the sun goes blank; comes to grief.
That face could be a focus for this back room,
For pack-rat papers strewn as if in rage,
Fond notes unread: each wary eye a phial
Unstoppered to let huge Melville out, to calm
The sea of pages; Melville in older age:
The grown man's sleepy defiance of denial.

Elixir

On Mao Shan did Tao Hongjing a fabulous
Pharmacopeia decree: of cinnabar
And orpiment, mica and malachite;
Dragon foetus, liquid gold, realgar, lead—

Ingesting which sent one to bed; and soon
To be one with earth and sky. You ate and went
Immortal, one of the cloudy sages of air;
Saw jasper mountains, found Peach Blossom Spring;
Rode with the starry crane. But they didn't. They—

Just died. A kind of suicide, assisted
By the swank of alchemy, rank faith in fancy's
Medicine: red bole, white lead, Six-One cement.

They breathed; poisoned by nostrums, they perished thinking
Untimely death was apotheosis.

The News and the Weather

Exotica

> The Tarot deck, originally a trick-taking card game, was invested
> with esoteric wisdom only in the late 18th century by a French
> occultist, Antoine de Gebelin, Protestant cleric and Freemason.

Back when we smoked and followed the occult,
Gurus of angst, we'd turn the lights down low
And read the Tarot pack. Joan was our nuncio
Of probable joy, the prophet to consult
For low-downs on the future. To exult
Was fate in the halcyon, sideburned '70s!
What we meant and other questions were a breeze;
Taking a medium's word felt so adult.
Later we learned those cups and wands, The Wheel
Of Fortune, The World, Judgment—all those trumps—
Had little to say; and that renowned Madame
Sosostris, clairvoyante, was daft to deal
Her wicked pack, a card game geared for chumps,
Drawing those colorized blanks on the world to come.

Denny

Roger D. Hansen

We sensed the words he used he didn't quite
Have meanings for. When he did well, we felt
He faltered where it didn't show, inside;
Yet forged ahead like a child who grows in the night,
Spellbound. He'd hang in there, for ice would melt
Under pressure, even a river of ice. He tried
Himself
       but now when he looks over his
Fine shoulder he sees—another self; two men
Competing there, and neither ever thanks
The other. He finds how slow a glacier is
After the ribbons and the promises

And father waiting on him, waiting again;
His years line up there in receding ranks
Like so many doubting Thomases.

Span

Wacko in Waco, that shadow government
At heaven's gate arising; Native American
Relic and microbrewery's stout, both made
Last month; bar-coded babies; an argument
In limos when Captain Button loved a man;
Rodenberry's orbit, holy Leary; tubs of Koolade,
Guyanan hemlock, fad they took for food
Not knowing to what mountain they were bound
In heady flight. Change was what was good

For others. For us the day was flower-crowned,
Blue primulas from the cold earth. God
Was in the seasons, a spellbound sun had found
Hosta to coax up; time, run down, had slowed
For the bud bulging, a hound sniffing a hound.

Albiani's

April 1997

I was walking west on 54th, New York,
1980, the man accosted me and said
Goodness, you're here, greetings on this street,
Dear Stephen! I turned, turned in the fresh torque
Of my day, it was Allen Ginsberg, his ready hand
Touching my shoulder, bearded thunderhead
Of gentleness above my parched conceit
And dimness; heat-lightning, brand
Fresh from the fire who never could forget;
Friend of everyone he ever met.

Remember that night in Albiani's, wired, live
With two more coffees, all others gone to bed,
We sang a prayer and shared another weed
Before the sun rose, Cambridge, 1965?

The Landscapes of Rubens

The left had to say greenhouse effect, loss
Of biodiversity, population crisis, uncontrollable
Disease, agricultural exhaustion, volcano
Eruptions. The right had to say asteroid,
Interstellar cloud, Arthur C. Clarke and explod-
ing supernova, disappearance of water,
Spontaneous ignition of the atmosphere.
They awoke from the complacency of solutions.

"I hear he died on the Côte d'Azur." "Yes,
About 90 when he died. His daughter was
The countess; *she* lived in Paris. These are people
Who made money in Cuba in the 19th century.
Tobacco, you must know. Now we will study
The landscapes of Rubens, quiet, yet charged with meaning."

Travertine

Gianni Versace

Watching the summer's death (by now, each season
Brings its own blockbuster butchery) I see how
His blood sank into the blond travertine
Of his own front steps; the smiling stone so
Smooth yet seamed, as if the point of it—that
Rugged look—was to trace the course of its decay.
Wrought iron gates, bars curling and bending, compose
A screen to protect the inside precinct and

Reveal it—neighbors die to be invited in. What
Was the crossing, the squaring, they found? Whatever it was
Surely it had to take place here, where envious
Stricken gazes and votive candles bloom. Blood
From the skull invests the pockets of the travertine
That soaks it up, holds it for all the world to see.

Astray

Driving along I thought the poet had some nerve
Bringing it up: so far off course, his own name
Mentioned—but where, in what context, what fame?
Like that gray from March-gray woods I had to swerve
To miss—sorry, shabby-coated beast—a coyote,
No doubt of it, but how far out of place
There on the empty highway! Thoughtless grace
All but got him whacked by my Toyota;
Unblinking, vagrant as poetry, a wild verve
In that reverted head, astray without his pack
As a word sung out of tune but sung out boldly!
Nothing to do with us, with business, or the curve
Of talk our evening get-together took,
We beheld his flash of self-absorption coldly.

Overhead

Now half asleep she heard the sonic boom
Knock her window, burly legerdemain;
She felt it in her bed, across the room,
Rattle the window pane
                once—and only once—as if
It did not ask but kicked the door with steel-toed boot
And took possession, one of the roughs: tough,
                vertiginous, destitute.
  The possession it announced was nothing final

No knock of Linz brimming with doom; but
As if new neighbors, after the flush and lull
Of first possession, stopped with shears and cut
The survey pins, re-drawing lines with braggadocio;
     entered to ogle —& dance their angry drag.

On First Looking for Hale-Bopp

Often I've traveled where sleepless hours unrolled
Like flatlands without end or origin;
On many midnight lookouts have I been
Which poets and crews of Dionysus hold
Precious in bright careers. So I've been told
How Vaughan beheld eternity, one night
Up late, great ring of pure and endless light.
Then on the Evening News I watched unfold

The tale of how a comet soon would pass.
I rose—as many a night by dreams undone
I've stared for stars—and North NE across
The cloudy night I peered into oblivion
Beyond my Baptist neighbor's neon cross;
And, silent, fell to sleep in Bennington.

Force of Nature

Facing the music of desires you
Forgot what would become of you; blew it
Like the Iceman climbing in the clamor of a blizzard.
On the Otztal Alp five thousand years ago.
Yearning was fuel; yet the white-out buried the climber,
His possessions, chalcolithic gear. The rest—
What trade, what life, what promise he was keeping,
What valley of satisfaction he pressed on to reach—

Puzzle us; we only see how he wanted to get
Somewhere, wanted but could not and gave back
Everything. No one knows where he was headed,
Why so forlorn, what it was all about;
Only that he, like you, had dealt with desire
As it was, a force of nature; and had lost.

Four Corners, Vermont

October sun, blue sky
burning the fields sienna,
even the governor upstate
raking a lawn, his kingdom
of this world. That afternoon
on Main Street, at the four
corners, the cop was trying
to push a small bat with
the butt of his pistol from
the window-box by the door
of the Putnam Hotel, an
unused window-box
where the bat, mistaken, caught
by daylight, had fluttered down
like a fallen leaf. Three
townsmen, not doing much
but holding their own, keeping
up on the news, kept watch.
The policeman laughed, tucking
his pistol back in its
holster. The teenage bellhop
so far with nothing to do
has pitched the bat out now.
It quavers to the walk
by the rail of the hotel stairs.
The bellhop and a man
wearing a jack shirt, worn
and too small for his arms,
stomp at it, grinding their heels
between the palings. The boy
runs back inside. It is
Norman Rockwell-ish, this
tableau the passers-by
are watching. Soon the boy
is back and kneeling with
a fork. The leaves have fallen
but the day is warm; even

the governor tidies his lawn.
The boy will jab at the black
remnant, the tines will ring
out, hitting the pavement
again; again. Everyone
in the land must know his place,
any beast
of the field his lair, his own.

The Water Spider

Dilatory cormorants, airing their heavy wings
like paltry aliens in capes, look shoreward
as mist burns upward, taking emerging landfall
in stride, sunlight skidding among their wings
                         spreading, unspreading.

Low tide, the sluggish ledges surface from the cove;
raw, dour and putrid, slick from the deep,
stray shards of Arnold's naked shingle: yet
a minor eminence above the tide supports
                         a rod of grass—

enough to be owned, but not enough to have
a name. The weedy brows come up for hours;
they belong to Mrs. Thompson while they're topside—
to be seen or stepped on. But how they are rooted, how
                         their tentacular

huddle of shelves lies in wait to lunge at a keel!
Men who warily skirt them from wharf to mooring
have wished them gone; lurking or gleaming, minimal
black alp at morning's neap or slant garden
                         of kelp and fucus

tossing awash as if to beckon, beckon
the dinghy's prow as it skates barely over them;
rising or resting inches below our keel.
Yet sunny mornings in July this year a launch
                         will cautiously put

one passenger ashore, a lady in a smock
and broadbrimmed hat, who carries her stool,
her case of water colors; sets her parasol
and settles in to sketch sky, cove, pine-hedged
                         granitic banks.

The cormorants, black adjutants, back off
but seem to follow every move of brush on pad
where water sways and calms and with the hours
mounts toward her place. As slabs of ledge dry off
                    in the sun she spreads

her sketches on the rocks to air, weighting them down
with loosened stones. She keeps on painting. Makes
her way down to the water to sketch a rock pool
and the water spider that makes its lobed shadow
                    fringed with colors

flash on the sunny bottom as it wins
its way grassward from cold eddies. Each day
a novelty, as out of mist rocks abruptly loom,
although from habit sailor or lobsterman knows
                    which way to head

having a sense of what he's aiming for, knowing
the way to miss this obstacle—inert, succinct,
not veined or crystal-flecked but black as any
ruin charred—only an elderly sketcher's
                    destination.